SHORT STORIES

BY

JAMES DALBY

PROLOGUE

Some of these stories are chapters taken from the books written by me, a few from a febrile imagination, and others are true stories of what happened. In all cases, I have indicated their origin.

It hopefully may tempt you to buy my books published on Amazon.

The front cover has no relation to the content of any of these stories, simply, that it reminded me of the area of Devon where we now live.

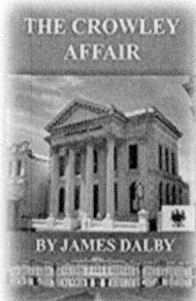
THE CROWLEY AFFAIR
BY JAMES DALBY

Sailing on Silver
By
James Dalby

THE CASTRATORS
BY JAMES DALBY

THE SHANGHAI INCIDENT
BY JAMES DALBY

THE SCOTTISH PREROGATIVE
THE WUHAN AFFAIR
JAMES DALBY

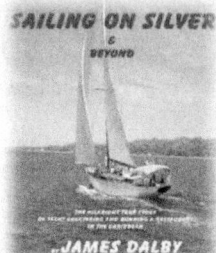
SAILING ON SILVER & BEYOND
...JAMES DALBY

MOSCOW ASSASSIN
BY JAMES DALBY

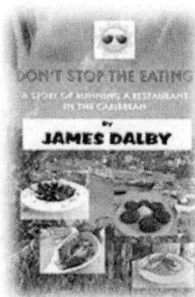
DON'T STOP THE EATING
A STORY OF RUNNING A RESTAURANT IN THE CARIBBEAN
BY
JAMES DALBY

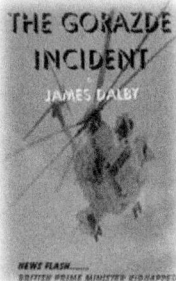
THE GORAZDE INCIDENT
JAMES DALBY
NEWS FLASH......
BRITISH PRIME MINISTER KIDNAPPED

A SHITTY DAY IN PARADISE
BY
JAMES DALBY

I AM WHO I AM
By:
JAMES DALBY

TABLE OF CONTENTS

5

THE BEGINNING

CHAPTER
1

"The punishment for rape should be castration."
— Amit Abraham

> *This is the first chapter of 'The Castrators,' a story initially based on Boko Haram in Nigeria, a country I know well having lived, worked, and travelled there. The story is fiction but the kidnapping of the 300 girls is factual.*
> *The story carries on to Crete and the Greek mainland where our heroes attempt to prevent Russia from expanding its influence in the eastern Mediterranean,*
> *where there is a link with the Islamic state.*

Doctor Farah Abubakar was late. She had left Maiduguri in the province of Borno in north-eastern Nigeria over an hour ago, heading for Chibok where she was the doctor in charge of the medical health of over 400 female students who boarded there. Farah liked to believe she was a modern Muslim and was proud of the fact the school was mixed with girls from all "lifestyles" and religions.

When initially offered the position two years ago, she was a staunch proponent of a mixed society living in peace together.

Thoughts ran through her head as she accelerated her old Land Rover Station Wagon across the interchange just north of the small town of Wuyaram. Only 40 minutes to go, she thought to herself. She mused about her background that had brought her to Chibok. Her grandfather, the first President of the newly formed Nigerian nation, had been a schoolteacher before entering politics.

Considered an honest man with great plans for the most populous country in Africa, he suffered what was to become an almost routine procedure for African Presidents during that time. Murdered in a coup before he had had a chance to put reforms into effect; the coup was organised by four Igbo army Majors and one Yoruba of the same rank. She remembered their plot failed and Major General Ironsi, a Christian and an Igbo snatched the initiative from their failure and took over the leadership of the country. She sighed as she recalled the story that led to yet another coup shortly afterwards when Yakubu Gowan came to power, and it became Ironsi's turn to suffer a similar fate.

At that stage, Gowan was only a Lieutenant Colonel, but because he was from the Tiv tribe situated in the north, it appeared Nigeria would settle down, he is being neither Igbo nor Muslim Hausa; two of the three major tribes, the third being the Yoruba. He was, however, a Christian, which perhaps laid the ground for yet more difficulties. The problems were not long in coming. The Igbo nation, situated in the south-east of the country, decided to separate from Federal Nigeria under their leader Colonel Ojukwu; the new state was named Biafra. Ojukwu should have realised, mused Farah, that secession of the state that had all the oil was a non-starter, and it set off one of the bloodiest civil wars in Africa's history ending in total defeat for the new nation state.

Ojukwu, forced to leave Nigeria after the collapse of Biafra, remained abroad for a decade but in a show of reconciliation, he returned and even stood for President in 2000. He died in 2012 treated as a hero of the nation at his burial.

Farah was so engrossed in her thoughts, she neglected to notice a large truck hurtling towards her in the middle of the narrow road, not an unusual occurrence in Nigeria. She took immediate action, which forced her to swerve into the bush narrowly missing a large tree. She thanked God she was driving a Land Rover, as a standard car would almost certainly have gone out of control. Once she was back on the tarmac road, she looked in the mirror and saw the truck, dust spilling out behind it, still in the middle of the road. It was then she recalled the sign on the front of the truck, "PEN IS MIGHTIER THAN SWORD". Her whole body was shaking but she started laughing uncontrollably as the space between PEN and IS was close together, giving quite a different meaning. Most trucks in Nigeria have a motif on the front, usually above the cab, and she was surprised she had the time to read it. Then she realised the two conflicting emotions were due to shock, so she pulled into the side of the road and stopped until she felt safe to drive again.

The rest of her trip was uneventful until she was about a kilometre from Chibok. It was the smell; deep and putrid, that first alerted her and as she looked at the sky, she saw a red glow followed by thick billowing smoke. Her first thought was a forest fire, but such fires were virtually non-existent in that part of Africa, particularly in the rainy season. She reached the outskirts of Chibok travelling down the main street and turning left after half a kilometre towards the school. Looking right, her heart seemed to reach her mouth. 'Oh my God,' she exclaimed aloud, realising it was the school buildings that were on fire. She stopped the Land Rover fearing the intensity of the heat might engulf her in the conflagration.

She frowned, as there was no sign whatsoever of any pupils or staff. The houses around the area were still smouldering, and dead bodies were lying in the short road toward the school. Climbing out of the Land Rover, she walked carefully towards the blazing inferno shielding her eyes from the intense heat, She was conscious of a movement in the grass in the garden of a house nearby. At first, she thought it was some sort of animal, but something told her the noise was human and one in considerable distress. She ran across the waist-high grass and almost tripped over the female form lying there. She recognised the girl immediately; she was a student from Calabar in eastern Nigeria. She was drenched in blood, and her clothes ripped, leaving her semi-naked. Farah's medical experience immediately clicked in, and she bent down to attend to the girl. After a quick investigation, it was evident that her condition was due to a brutal rape, and she had a nasty wound on one of her breasts. The girl was shaking and hysterical. Farah calmed her before running to the Land Rover. She got in and quickly drove it over the thick foliage to where the girl lay.

Grabbing her medical bag, she ran over, gave her a sedative injection, and then looked at the wounds. She realised they were too severe to be treated properly on the spot, but she managed to stem the blood flow as best she could but was worried there may be internal bleeding, which would need urgent attention.

The school was about a kilometre from Chibok Hospital and Farah was torn between seeing if there were other casualties needing help, and getting the girl to the hospital, but realising the urgency she chose the latter option. She half-carried and half-dragged the student into the back of the Station Wagon and laid her down as best she could. The girl was now shivering with shock despite the intense heat of the day. She covered her with an old blanket she kept in the back in case of a breakdown and jumped into the driving seat, driving back down the road towards Chibok. Her passenger was moaning softly while she drove, but Farah knew, as the girl was semi-conscious it was unlikely, she was suffering any pain especially since the sedative would have taken effect.

As she drove toward the hospital grounds, she noticed many people milling around the external walls. A police officer stopped her before entering the road leading to the hospital.

"You can't go in there's been a disaster at Kiyak." Farah knew Kiyak was a village not far from Chibok.

"Well constable, there's also been a disaster at the Government Secondary School, it's been burned down, and I suspect there are many casualties. I'm a doctor and have a desperately ill patient in the back."

The police officer looked in the back of the Station Wagon. 'I'm sorry, but I've instructions not to let any more people in...'

Farah let out a snort and gunned the engine. As she reached the emergency entrance, she saw a man she recognised, it was Doctor Joseph Spencer, a British general surgeon attached to the Chibok hospital by Medicines sans Frontières, his apron was splashed with blood. Just as Farah caught his attention, the police officer caught up with the Station Wagon and started shouting that she had to leave. The shouting caught Joe Spencer's attention, and he ran over. "Leave this woman alone," he said forcefully, "She's a doctor, and God knows what we could do with her help here." The police officer looked uncertain, but Farah ignored him.

"Joe, there has been some sort of disaster at the school, when I arrived there the place was in flames. I did not see any other casualties, only dead bodies, but heard the cries of this poor girl in the back. She has clearly lost a lot of blood from a brutal rape and a deep wound to a breast. I've tried to patch her up and given her a sedative, but I suspect she may have internal bleeding."

Joe walked around to the rear of the vehicle and gestured to two medical orderlies who had just come out of the hospital for some fresh air. "Get this girl straight into the operating theatre, and I'll follow in a few seconds." He turned to Farah. "I will see to her straight away, but if you can help the staff here, there are many with wounds that are not life-threatening, we are completely overwhelmed. I've telephoned the military to get medical helicopters here so we can spread the load, but surprise, surprise, fuck all has happened," he said bitterly. "Unless we can get some of the injured to other hospitals, there are going to be many more deaths."

"Of course, I'll help," she said, torn between going back to the school area to see if there were more live causalities or dealing with the current situation in front of her. Joe gave his thanks and disappeared into the hospital, saying he would meet her later.

Farah followed him, seeing some wounded people in the hospital lobby that included women and children as well as men, although there seemed to be more of the former. She realised what Joe had said was an understatement; the staff at the small hospital could not possibly manage without help. She suddenly had an idea and pulled out her mobile phone punching in a number. Frustratingly there was no answer. She was about to put the phone back in her bag when it rang.

"Hi Farah," said the cheery voice, "I was in the shower when you called, but recognised the number, how are you?"

"I desperately need your help Chizzy," (her full name was Chiziterem, but she was always referred to as Chizzy). She recognised a sense of panic in her friend's voice.

"What's the problem Farah, you sound terribly upset?"

Farah told her all she knew. "It appears there's been an attack on a local village as well as the school, I assume by Islamists, but I can't be sure of those facts, all I know is the hospital here can't cope, and God knows how many casualties there are from the school..."

"Okay, has anyone called the army...?"

"Yes, apparently Joe Spencer the local surgeon here called both the governor's office and the military for helicopters, but nothing seems to have been done. Your uncle is now the President, and I am wondering if..."

Chizzy cut her off. "Farah, you leave everything to me, I'll deal with it from here. Try to assess for me how much help you need for the casualties you're aware of and call me back, in the meantime, I'll start the ball rolling. Oh, and do not go back to the school whatever you do, there may be some nasties still around. You do what you can at the hospital, and we will work together to sort out the problem." Farah smiled to herself. Chizzy was a lawyer with a Harvard degree; nothing ever seemed to faze her. She knew Chizzy positively loved to be at the centre of things; there was no doubt matters would shortly start to hum.

She went over and talked to the nursing staff and some of the doctors. They told her there were fifteen people, who were seriously injured either with gunshot or knife wounds, and waiting to be treated, but Joe was the only surgeon available, and they explained that there was only one operating theatre. She called Chizzy back. "Hi Chizzy, I reckon fifteen serious and thirty-five or so that need attention. The problem is as quickly as people are seen to; more arrive."

"Okay Farah, I've arranged for several army medical helicopters all with medical staff, they should be with you shortly. If someone could put sheets out on a flat piece of ground indicating an 'H' as near the hospital as possible that would help them land, make sure there are no overhead wires... Now I'm told there's also a company of the 1st Battalion on the way to you by road, and they'll also have medics with them, but I've told them to go straight to the school area to see if there are survivors."

"That's great Chizzy, you're a wonder. I will go now with some bed sheets and peg them to the ground outside. Talk to you later."

Farah asked a male nurse to help her, and soon there was a large "H" pegged to the ground with meat skewers. She checked for overhead wires, there were none.

As she went back into the hospital, she saw her doctor friend emerging from the operating theatre; he looked tired and sweaty.

"Is Chi Ekpo, okay?"

"Oh, that's her name I'll let the nurses know. Thanks to you, she will live. I reckon another half hour, and she'd have bled to death."

"Why was there a wound on her breast?" asked Farah puzzled.

"Ah, yes, it was quite deep. What these bastards do is they cut off the breasts after the raping. They must've been disturbed or called away; God these people are the worst type of depraved humanity you can imagine."

Farah shuddered. 'Well, it's good news she'll pull through.'

"Yes, but the mental damage will take much longer to repair, poor girl, the problem is there is never any justice for these people to bring about closure. There is another issue and that is that the families of raped girls disown them and their children. So not only do they suffer abuse, but they're in effect blamed for being raped." It was at this point they heard helicopters. John Spencer looked up at the sky in surprise.

"I haven't been idle,' smiled Farah. 'I called a great friend of mine who has influence, and the result is choppers, There's also an Army team with medics on the way, although I think the latter is probably due to your original call, they'll move down to the school to see if there are any survivors."

"You are a beauty, Farah," John hugged her with tears in his eyes. "I'll get the staff to start preparing for some of the more seriously injured to be flown out," he turned, and half ran back into the building.

For the next few hours, Farah helped the team at the hospital, and because it was dark when she finally finished, she accepted a makeshift bed to catch a few hours' sleep. By that time, she had received a report from the school, regarding the kidnapping of many students.

As she lay in bed going over the day's events, she made a firm resolution. Not only was she going to rebuild the school but also, somehow, she would think of a way to deal with the murderous band that had caused such mayhem. She woke in the middle of the night with a plan but had no idea at this stage how to put it into effect.

TIME

CHAPTER
2

"Reality is an illusion brought about
In the absence of alcohol"

> *This is from my book 'I Am Who I Am'. It suggests that time is going backward instead of our perception of it going forward.*
>
> *The story starts with a monk who comes to the door and TIME is one of the earlier chapters.*

"We touched upon a time when we were discussing reality earlier, but I have often wondered what time is."

Father Paul looked surprised. "Do you mean whether it is real or unreal, your perception or that of another?"

"Oh, I perceive time as a very personal thing in that it can appear to go more quickly for me than the next man if I am busy and he is not, or more slowly if the reverse is the case. But that perception of time speeding up and slowing down is the mind because a clock would confirm that time was the same for both people."

"That's true, but only if the physical you is in the same space, if space is different, time can change between the two depending upon their speed of travel."

"I understand that, but for time to function it must

15

have one other factor."

"Remind me," said Father Paul.

"Time must have space, otherwise, nothing could move, and time must also have movement. Otherwise, there is no time, space on its own is not time, but space and movement together are time, in other words, they are one, as has been proved by Einstein."

"Yes, that seems to be a logical conclusion," said Father Paul, we know that we perceive the solar system to be moving rather rapidly outwards in what we call space, so time is the product of that. What you do not quite understand, is that time warps within space and in theory may reverse itself if the movement of the object goes faster than the speed of light, although physicists tell us that nothing can go faster than the speed of light. This, in fact, is not entirely correct, subatomic particles called tachyons, if they exist, travel faster than light. As you are interested in poetry, here is one for you."

A rocket explorer named Wright,

Once travelled much faster than light,

He set out one day, in a relative way,

And returned on the previous night!

Anonymous

"There is also another phenomenon. The quantum theory permits objects to influence each other instantaneously even when on the other side of the universe. So, current science is still largely ignorant about what can be achieved. It seems that rules thought to be absolute, may be able to be broken."

"Yes, this is where I struggle to understand how time could move backwards," I said, "having read that if the solar system stopped its expansion and started to track back

16

towards the point of the big bang, assuming there was such a thing, everything would work backwards. The cup you dropped a few minutes ago, would spring together again. But that somehow seems illogical."

Father Paul smiled. "Well in our current conversation if what we see is reality, which we have already agreed may not be the case, let us make another assumption, perhaps time is circular. Everything else appears to be in the solar system, indeed in the universe, from the smallest particles such as atoms to the largest stars, so why not time?"

I frowned. "If time were circular, what would that mean?"

"Well for a start, it would mean that the universe would not fall back on itself or continue to expand to infinity, it would simply continue to turn on an axis, rather like the Earth around the sun."

"In such a scenario, this could suggest what has happened once would happen again, and again, and again?"

Father Paul took another sip of water. "Not necessarily, the earth goes around the sun, but we don't start life again at the end of each year unless you're a plant, but if you assume that in a reversal situation, time goes backward, and if time is circular, the earth will eventually return to where it started. But without the cataclysmic coming together that the Big Bang suggests, and then the process would start all over again. Your perception of going forward will always remain. Perhaps we continue experiencing a merry-go-round until we find a way off," he laughed.

"How would that affect time travel?" I asked.

"Well, I am not a physicist," said Father Paul, "but it seems to me that if time is curved, then by going in a straight line at a determined speed, you may be able to take a shortcut either to the past or the future."

I smiled. "But which future and which past?"

Father Paul shook his head.

"Another thing about time travel that has always bemused me, is the thought of going back and meeting myself." I was astonished by Father Paul's roar of laughter.

"What's so funny?" I asked.

"Forgive me," he said, "but I somehow found that thought rather amusing. Let us just consider such a proposal for a minute. If you could travel back through time and meet yourself as a younger man, and let's just assume for the discussion that the time situation you have chosen is the correct one, what would you experience and what would that experience tell you?"

I thought deeply for a minute. "Well, the person I met would not be me because I could not be conscious of being within two bodies at the same time," I paused. "What I would be seeing is an image of what I was, a living image admittedly, but an image just the same."

"And what would that suggest?" asked Father Paul.

"It could suggest several things, for instance, it could suggest that a permanent image is left behind, or that there are infinite copies of the universe, or that there are infinite dimensions. It is accepted that the new quantum computer, although in its infancy, maybe utilising copies of itself in other universes to enable it to carry out calculations in seconds that could otherwise take thousands of years to answer."

"But what about the future?"

"Hmm, well if the same principle were to operate for the future as well as the past, it would be difficult to have an image of me in the future, or would it?" My mind started spinning at the possibilities. "The only possibility is that the image of me is set in time forever and that my experience within the image is illusory so that if I went backward or forwards in time to meet myself, I would not be meeting me, but an image of my current illusion. This would then tend to firm up the argument that there is no choice."

"Not necessarily," said Father Paul, "as you may

change the future, the change may be infinitesimal, but the choice is still there, as we discussed."

"Yes, I suppose that would not matter, and yet if I went back to my image as a young man and told him of the errors I was about to make, I may change his complete understanding and thus his future. Then what would that do to my memory?"

"It would not change because you would be addressing your image, and not yourself. If it were the arrogant young man that, was you, he probably wouldn't listen anyway."

Father Paul waited for my reaction, but I just smiled.

"If he did change," continued Father Paul, "It would not affect you because you have moved past that point and there would be a diversity of purpose."

"You mean that a different universe would be created?"

"Hmm, possibly, but on the other hand, we cannot discount the fact that as you proceed in life, your vibrations change and thus if you went back in time, it may be that while you could watch your image as it was, that image would be unaware of you. In other words, it would be a living three-dimensional being etched in time forever, but for all practical purposes rather than a celluloid image. Indeed, you cannot discount the idea that time itself is a pulse that switches off and on in tune with the vibrations of matter, rather like the frame of a film, thus it may be possible to slice time like a sausage."

I visualised time as a sausage being cut up, but I stopped when the vision became too ludicrous to consider.

Father Paul held his hand up as I was about to speak. "I have another proposal for you."

"Go on," I smiled.

"Let us look at Einstein's Theory of Relativity. You will remember that it was simply explained by the two trains standing in the station. If you were sitting in the stationary train, and the other train moved out of the station, on the assumption that you could not see anything else but the train you were sitting in and be aware that one train was moving, you would not know which train."

"I remember, and it is certainly true, as I have experienced the illusion."

"I am glad you call it an illusion, for that, is indeed what it is. But let us now take that theory a little further. We will name the train you are sitting in as Perceptive Reality, PR for short."

I nodded.

"The other train we will call Time. Now we assume it is night, and there are no lights in the station, so we are unaware of anything else but the two trains."

"Okay," I said as I mentally adjusted my vision of the two trains.

Father Paul looked at me. "Let us leave the trains for one moment. Would you agree that what we perceive in life, is that we run concurrently with time, in other words, time and ourselves appear to move in a forward direction, from the past to the future?"

"Yes of course," I agreed.

"Back to the train then," he smiled, "now let us assume in Scenario 1 that both the PR train and the TIME train move out of the station at the same time and at the same speed and in the same direction. What would your perception be?"

I frowned, providing the carriage was very well insulated for noise, it would appear to be stationary I answered because there would be no yardstick in which to measure movement." I wondered where Father Paul was moving to in the discussion, and then it came to me in a flash.

"Exactly," he said, seeing my expression of understanding. "This means that in our PR train, our perception of reality, we would have no movement when viewed against time. Now we know that is not the case, because we perceive, that we are moving in time."

"Yes, that is correct."

"Taking your Sherlock Holmes method of deduction, therefore, it appears that there are three other possibilities. In scenario 2 the PR train is moving forwards and the TIME train is stationary so the perception of the observer on the PR train would be that either the TIME train was moving forwards (in the other direction) or the PR train was moving forwards (In the opposite direction). In reality (not in perception), the TIME train would be stationary, and the PR train would be moving forward. However, in our perception time does not stand still while we move forward.

"Now," Father Paul continued, "let us look at the other two scenarios. The TIME train moves forward (in the opposite direction) out of the station at the same time as the PR train moves forward (in the opposite direction). The perception of the observer on the PR train would be that either the PR train was moving forward (in the opposite direction) or that the TIME train was moving forward (in the opposite direction). Both trains would be moving but in different directions.

"In the final scenario, the TIME train moves forward out of the station, and the PR train stands still. The observer on the PR train would perceive either the TIME train is moving (in the opposite direction), or the PR train is moving (in the opposite direction), but, the observer would be standing still.

"We know we appear to be moving forward with time, but whichever way you observe from the two trains in the station, the only way you could see the TIME train and PR train moving together in the same direction would appear in scenario 1, where to the observer it would seem that both were stationary. If we perceive we are moving then time is either stationary or moving backward, so why do we take the view that time is moving forward. The only answer to that is because we sense we are moving forwards, we assume time

21

is moving in the same direction, but that may not be the case."

I was getting dizzy, "what you are saying is that our perception of reality may be wrong. In your argument, it could be that we are standing still or moving forward in the opposite direction from time."

"Yes, in the example I have just shown you, we perceive we are going forwards but in the other direction from time,"

"How do we know which is forward and which is backward" I asked.

Father Paul smiled. "We don't, but the example I have put to you just suggests that time and ourselves could be travelling in different directions or that either TIME train or PR could be standing still.

"I am not, of course, suggesting that Einstein was incorrect he was simply giving two trains as an example to explain relativity. What I have done is simply extrapolate the movement of those trains to suggest that we may not be able to tell whether the time is going in the same direction, as we perceive."

(Later I designed a diagram, which follows this chapter to make it easier to follow).

I nodded, yes, if that were not the case, we would appear to be stationary, and that is certainly not our perception. This could suggest that our future is, in fact, our past, and further demonstrates that time may be curved or cyclic, in that everything that happens has happened before."

"Back to the '*déjà Vu* feeling," I laughed, "but what happens when time leaves the station, and we are left standing there?"

"Then perhaps your perception of reality has ended, and you are stationary without time, but still within space. The '*I am*' is still conscious as to what is, without the illusion. Perhaps now the time train has left the station we will be able to see what is on the other side, indeed perhaps the station lights can be switched on so that we understand what is there. Now, it may be that the next train into the station will recreate the perception of movement once again, but because this train arrives after the previous one, the perception of time will be relative to the two trains. Thus, although the perception of reality will be similar when the second train moves out of the station, it will be different because the time train will be later, and thus your perception of time will have moved too."

"That is certainly an interesting theory," I said, as my brain raced to take in the implications of what Father Paul was suggesting. "What you are suggesting is that we are travelling forward into the past."

"Yes, but here is another possibility,"

"Go on," I smiled.

"When the second TIME train appears at the station and then leaves, that could create another perception of reality which could be reincarnation."

"Yes, and the third, fourth, and so on, when does it all end?" I asked.

"It may not end, but be a constant journey, perhaps when you realise you are not going any further with your perceived reality, you will get off the train."

I laughed, "Perhaps we are waiting for the station lights to be illuminated so that we can find our way." Then I thought of another idea. "There is another possibility."

"Oh?' Father Paul looked at me seriously.

"If time is curved, which we know that both time and space are, and the TIME train originally sets off into the future, it will then eventually curve around to the past while the '*I am*' is sitting in the future. In which case what we may be experiencing now is a past life. This would mean of course that any travel into the past from our present position would be an illusion within my illusion." My mind tried to grasp the possibilities.

23

Father Paul smiled. "There is no doubt that the future and the past may be one reality. Indeed, we could not arguably have a future unless someone had conceived the idea first because we have agreed that everything comes from the mind, either our own or God's, the first being your preference. But don't get too enthusiastic about my suggestions, as I have told you I am not a physicist, but our perception of being anchored to Earth means that it is sometimes difficult for us to separate what is real and what is not real. For instance, we are circling the sun, but we could just as easily say we are going forwards towards the sun in summer and backward in winter."

I nodded, part of my mind was hanging on to Father Paul's theory and the possibilities it created, while I broached the next subject.

"What about astrology?" I asked. "We are led to believe by some that the stars govern our lives."

Father Paul nodded. "What is your view?"

I compressed my lips. "I think I indicated earlier that I never discount anything unless I know it to be untrue. Many mysteries in life appear to have some substance, but as soon as you find a basis for the argument, someone produces an equally good argument that it was incorrect. I am a Scorpio, and I have observed that fellow Scorpios often have similar characteristics to me."

"You mean jealousy, lack of trust in others, inflated egos, arrogance..." I stopped Father Paul from his listing.

"No," I joked, "generosity, honesty, hard work, caution, intuition..."

"So, what does that tell you?"

"It doesn't say anything, unfortunately, but it does suggest there may be more to astrology than meets the eye. For instance, does it simply mean that the forces of the stars have a material effect on our characteristics, like the moon has a major effect on the tides, or to be a little more fanciful, does it mean that the person born within Scorpio comes

24

originally from that area of the solar system? Perhaps that is where my *station* is? I hope not, incidentally, because my wife is a Leo.

"It is a fact that there are at least thirteen astrological signs, not twelve, and that we are in effect working on star signs that are at least two thousand years old, so one can be somewhat cynical about the predictions made on what appears to be a false premise.

"I have also noticed that while horoscopes in the Western world are generally framed around what is good for you, those in the East are completely the opposite, but that may be because of the differing philosophies."

"Yes, the latter because Buddhists believe we come to Earth to suffer, not to have a good time."

"Back to my penal system idea," I grinned.

"Not just that," said Father Paul seriously, "but it does tend to highlight the point some people have about the Far East taking over from the West. Their perception is very different as to what life is all about, and while capitalism is now accepted by the Far East, their approach in a few cases is entirely different in that the workforce is appreciated and there is a responsibility for their welfare, rather like an extended family system. If the people of the Far East are wise, the capitalist system could be used for the well-being of the people, rather than the enrichment of the few, and it could work. Now, power politics is tending to negate such a policy, particularly in India and China."

"Don't forget," I said, "that George Peabody, an American philanthropist in the nineteenth century, created homes for poor people at affordable rents, and his legacy lives on today. Bill and Malinda Gates are using their wealth to help poor people in the world, so capitalism has and is being used for charitable purposes, it is simply that only a few wealthy people take this road.

"However, the idea of young men being encouraged to become Buddhist monks for a couple of years is a good one, particularly if they have no trade or no job to go to. Perhaps

25

there is some merit for the Far East taking over the world after all."

Father Paul laughed, "it would be a complete turnaround wouldn't it, the idea of anyone taking over someone is an anathema to me. But moving back to our discussion on whether there is truth within astrology, it strikes me that there are similar clues to our existence which are there to see.

"One is a hypnotic regression, and in fact, there have been cases of people being regressed into the future too. There is ample evidence of near-death experiences, and whatever one thinks about them, most who have experienced a near-death phenomenon, come back completely unafraid of the future, which tends to suggest that once one has faced one's fears, then fear of death is no longer a factor."

"Then there is spiritualism," I said.

"Ah yes, spiritualism and all that goes with it, what is your view of spiritualism James?"

"I was apparently christened in a spiritualist church," I said, "so you could say that I was brought up on it. My mother at one time was Catholic and my father a Methodist created quite a mixture for me to assimilate as a young person. I do not discount the possibility of us being able to contact those who have transcended to other areas, but I have a healthy scepticism, and because there are so many charlatans around, it's hard to discriminate between what is true and what is not true. Like the other things we have discussed, the spirit or energy exists, and if we believe we transcend elsewhere, then we cannot completely eradicate the thought of returning to what we term as spirit form or pure energy to talk to those we love. On the other hand, there may be good reasons why we would not wish to do so, and as time on earth as we perceive it, is like a microcosm in the oceans of reality, life may be akin to a ten-minute slumber, or less. (See my book 'The Crowley Affair'). Who knows? If that is the case, I see real difficulties in a meaningful connection between one reality and the next, and the truth may be local vibrations, telepathic vibrations, if you like,

26

picked up from the person looking for solace. Ghosts could quite easily be similar, in that a vision or feeling of reality is left behind by the being, particularly in the case of painful or frightening deaths. As discussed earlier, the fact that we can only be sure of one thing and that is being conscious of being here now, may mean that everything is an illusion and nothing is real, including time, space or indeed the whole human race."

Father Paul rocked gently on his heels which were now tucked away underneath his robe. He was nodding slowly, and I was surprised that he moved on to the next subject without commenting further.

He lifted his head and made a gesture with his right hand that indicated our philosophical discussion was over for the moment.

"I would now like to move us out of the realm of perceived reality," he said. "What do you think of religion?"

"Which religion are we discussing?" I asked.

"You tell me."

"My perception is that human beings have generally delegated responsibility for both their spiritual and political well-being, to such an extent, that they are now reaping the problems that policy has created."

"Very well then why don't you start with that point, and then move on to specifics afterward?"

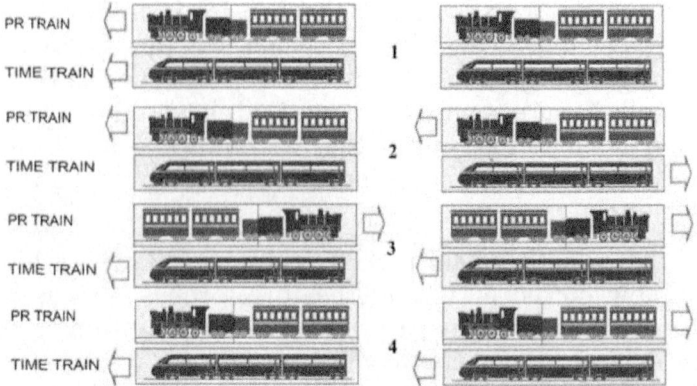

	REALITY		PERCEPTION

1. STATIONARY OR MOVING FORWARD TOGETHER

COMMENT: THE PERCEPTION IS THAT TIME IS STANDING STILL WHICH WE KNOW IT ISN'T.

2. THE PR TRAIN IS MOVING FORWARD AND THE TIME TRAIN IS STANDING STILL

COMMENT: THE PERCEPTION IS THAT EITHER THE PR TRAIN IS MOVING FORWARD OR THE TIME TRAIN IS MOVING FORWARD IN THE OTHER DIRECTION.
WE DO NOT PERCEIVE THAT TIME TRAVELS IN THE OPPOSITE DIRECTION AS THEN IT WOULD BE TRAVELLING BACKWARDS.

3. THE PR TRAIN IS TRAVELLING BACKWARDS AND THE TIME TRAIN IS TRAVELLING FORWARDS IN THE OTHER DIRECTION.

COMMENT: THE PERCEPTION IS THAT THE PR TRAIN IS TRAVELLING IN THE OPPOSITE DIRECTION TO THE TIME TRAIN WHETHER THE LATTER IS MOVING IN THE OTHER DIRECTION OR STANDING STILL.

4. THE PR TRAIN IS STANDING STILL WHILE THE TIME TRAIN MOVES FORWARD.

COMMENT: THE PERCEPTION IS THAT THE TIME TRAIN IS MOVING IN THE OPPOSITE DIRECTION TO THE PR TRAIN.

CONCLUSION: YOU = IN THE PR TRAIN PERCEPTION IS EITHER STANDING STILL OR MOVING IN A DIFFERENT DIRECTION TO TIME. BECAUSE WE ASSUME WE ARE MOVING FORWARD IN TIME, THIS SUGGESTS WE COULD IN FACT BE MOVING BACKWARDS, THE OPPOSITE TO OUR PERCEPTION.

THE WEDDING

CHAPTER
3

"For better or for worse, often
depends on circumstances".

This is a chapter from 'Sailing on Silver' Part II, when we
were running a restaurant in the Caribbean. It is also in a
separate book called 'Don't Stop the Eating'.

Many Caribbean islands offer Europeans and
Americans an all-in holiday that includes a marriage service
as well as a honeymoon. Interestingly, although most of
these marriages are second or third attempts, we came
across several couples who were getting married for the first
time. Because their families were not usually present, I was
occasionally asked if I would be the best man. The last time I
agreed to do this proved to be rather more memorable than
I had thought possible.

Bob and Susie Hall had been one of our first
customers at the Pub when they were in St Lucia on holiday.
We liked them both. Susie was a vivacious blonde and lots of
fun, while Bob had a dry sense of humour. He reminded me
of the 'Bob' in the Likely Lads, a comedy program on the
BBC.

Six months later they returned, coming to see us on
the first day after their arrival. They told us that they had
decided after several years of living together, to get married.

Susie had seen an advertisement in their local newspaper about special marriage deals in certain St Lucian hotels, and as they had enjoyed their previous stay on the island, they settled for St Lucia again. They both asked us if we would help, and Bob asked if I would be his best man, as his best friend could not make the trip from England. It was agreed that the wedding buffet be held at the Pub, and as none of their relatives were coming for the wedding, they said they would invite fellow guests from the hotel to make up the numbers. They reckoned the party would not be more than about twenty, people. (It turned out to be nearer fifty).

Usually, the minister was brought to the hotel to officiate the wedding, but Susie was keen to get married in church, so on Monday morning I took her up to meet the vicar at Gross Islet who was delighted to agree to perform the ceremony, which was set for the following Saturday.

Susie had not brought a dress out with her, so Liz flew up with her to Martinique where they found exactly what she required. Liz found a lot of other clothes that she assured me she required too, so all in all, it was an expensive trip for both. When they returned, slight alterations had to be carried out to Susie's wedding dress, and there was a general feeling of excitement building up with the Pub's staff, as the day drew near.

Susie was particularly keen to be driven away from the church in something other than a motor car. She had made some enquiries at the hotel, and they advised her that the riding school nearby might be able to help her, as they had some traps (two-wheeled buggies) that they may consider hiring out. When I heard of the idea, I was a little dubious, as I knew that the horses from this school were somewhat wild. Susie was insistent however, so I suggested that they hire an experienced driver, but she would have none of it, so we arranged for a horse and trap to be delivered to the church after the service.

I spent a good deal of time with Bob, so that I could glean enough information to provide a reasonable best man's speech, and it was during this time that he indicated he wanted to have a stag night on Friday, the day before the wedding. He had invited several new-found friends he had met at the hotel, and it was decided that we would eat at a restaurant on the other side of town and then gravitate to the (then) only nightclub in Rodney Bay called Lucifer's which was part of the St Lucian hotel.

Liz arranged a hen night for Susie at the Pub, which was inevitably going to be somewhat less boisterous, at least that was the general idea.

Friday evening came, and I picked Bob and two of his new-found friends up from the hotel, the others followed in a taxi. We had a reasonable meal and plenty to drink, so by the time we got to Lucifer's, we were all in good spirits.

Lucifer's was situated in a large basement of the hotel, and the whole of the inside had been transformed to look like an underground cavern with seats and tables inside smaller caves, which was supposed to give a degree of privacy. Other than that, it was like any other disco worldwide, in that it had flashing coloured lights and was otherwise darkened. There was a small stage where impromptu acts were carried out, and the billing for that evening was Queen Aphrodite. We knew Aphrodite (Aphro for short) quite well; she was a mature woman of indeterminate years, but still with an excellent figure. She would occasionally pick up men in the Pub, but although we quite liked her, she was not encouraged to use the restaurant as her stamping ground for obvious reasons. I had heard that she was a very good belly dancer but had never seen her perform until that night.

As she walked into the club, despite the darkness and the supposed privacy of the 'caverns' Aphro spotted me immediately and came over, she had her usual wig on which was black and set in a huge bouffant of dark curly hair, but underneath her short jacket I could see she had little else on. I introduced her to the party and told her that Bob was on his stag night. I wished I had not done so, as I saw the gleam in her eyes as she looked at him.

The show was quite good. Aphro managed to get up to all sorts of gyrations, and while being saucy was not over the top. It was obvious however, that the thirty-minute display was meant to impress only one person, Bob. To say that he was affected by Aphro's interest would be an understatement, and by the time she came back to the table, this time without coat, and wearing the flimsiest of garments, Bob was in a high state of expectancy.

As Aphro sat down at our table on Bob's knees, there followed some smooching and canoodling, which started to get more than a little embarrassing, as both Aphro and Bob appeared to be letting their passions run away with them. I decided to spoil their fun by reminding Bob where he was, and that he was getting married to Susie the next day.

All that managed to do, however, was to heighten Bob's desire, and he asked one of his new-found friends if he could borrow his hotel room. At first, the man refused, but after Aphro suggested that it need not just be a one-on-one affair, the man changed his mind and they all staggered off together. I just hoped that Susie didn't happen to be in the hotel lobby when they arrived there.

I stayed about another ten minutes or so, but as various 'ladies of the night' kept approaching our table, I decided it was time for me to go. It was a short walk from Lucifer's to the house, and I was surprised to see that there were already lights on when I arrived. When I got in, Liz and Susie were having coffee.

As Liz made me some coffee, we swapped stories about the evening with me leaving out the more obviously embarrassing bits and trying to keep Susie engaged in staying where she was. It didn't work for too long, and she stood up saying she must get back, as poor Bob would be waiting for her. Some hope I thought, as I stood up with her and offered to escort her across the road.

After giving me a quick perfunctorily goodnight kiss, Susie disappeared into the hotel, and I returned home. I didn't know the room number of Bob's friend, and as I did not know the other man's last name either, I could not warn Bob that Susie was back. Besides, I told myself, he was big enough to look after himself, and while being best man, it was hardly my job to interfere with his private life.

Liz was furious when I told her and said that I must go back to the hotel and try to find him. I was in two minds when our phone rang, as it was after 2.30 in the morning, I knew it could only be from one person.

I picked up the handset. "Yes?"

"James, it's Susie, do you know where Bob is? He's not here, and the bed has not been slept in. I'm worried," she added.

"Oh, I shouldn't worry, Susie..." I yelped as Liz kicked my shin. "He's probably in one of the bars..."

"No, he isn't," replied Susie, "I've looked everywhere, James you don't think..."

I wasn't sure quite what she was going to say, but I stopped her. "No, I am sure he's fine, he was with one of the other guys..."

"Which one?" She asked.

"Er, the chap called William, he has blond hair and..." I could have kicked myself as I said it.

"Oh, you mean William Bullock, thanks James, I'll find out his room number and see if Bob is..."

I swallowed my second cup of coffee the wrong way and had a coughing fit.

Liz raised her eyebrows and gave me a hefty swipe on the back.

"No, no don't do that" I spluttered out, with a strangled gasp, "William could be in bed without any clothes on" I added weakly. "I'll come around and knock him up myself."

"Oh, James, would you? I'm so sorry, I'll meet you in the lobby." With that she put the phone down.

Liz had sat close, listening to the telephone conversation. "Problems?" She asked, sweetly.

I scowled at her and told her what I was going to do.

"What if he's still with Aphro?" asked.

"Well, I'll just have to separate them, and somehow get Bob back to his room without Susie finding out," I smiled as I started to imagine what I might find.

As I was walking out, Liz called after me. "Oh, and tell Aphro from me, if you're not back in ten minutes flat, I shall be over there with a bloody machete."

"She's not my type, I answered truthfully."

I got to the lobby of the hotel to find Susie waiting for me. She had already woken up the scowling night receptionist and had got William's room number. I realised that there was no way that Susie was going to let me go alone, and perhaps her woman's intuition had already alerted her. I hoped to God that Aphro had left by the time we got there.

The room number was 113 at the end of a long passageway, which led out into the rear garden of the hotel. I knocked hard, and shouted that it was me and Susie, I emphasised the Susie, and said we were looking for Bob. I heard some grumbling going on inside, and then William swung the door open. He was naked from the waist up, but had some trousers on, which judging by the undone belt had been hastily pulled up.

"Bloody glad you've come, I can't get a bloody wink of sleep with these two shaggers," he saw Susie for the first time, as she pushed past me into the room. "Oh, bloody hell," said William.

There were two double beds in the room, one had obviously been used by William, the other contained Bob who was lying on his stomach, and Aphro, who I was amazed to see, was completely bald without her wig, slipping quickly out of the bed. She smiled at Susie, as she retrieved her wig. I thought it rather amusing that she should pick the wig to put on first because she had nothing else on. She smiled again at Susie, who had stopped in full flight, and was staring at the seemingly unconscious form of Bob. "Don't worry dearie," said Aphro, as she slipped on her sparse clothing, "he's not half bad... for a honkey," with that she glided past me and was gone.

"You bastards," screamed Susie, "you rotten bastards" She raised her handbag and brought it down on the back of Bob's unfortunate head. Bob who had no doubt buried his head in the pillow in a desperate attempt not to be noticed, let out a yelp of pain.

Susie then picked the large lamp off the bedside table and threw it at Bob just as he turned to fend off another handbag attack. The heavy brass object hit him on the upper cheek, and he let out another howl of pain.

Susie stamped out, and as she passed me to go through the door, she snarled, "It's your fault you bloody well led him to this." I watched for the swinging handbag, but she carried on through into the corridor. A split second later, she poked her head back into the room and shouted, "And the

34

bloody wedding's off." With that, she ran off in floods of tears.

"Oh shit," I said.

I looked at Bob, who already had the makings of an extremely bad black eye, and I suggested he get some ice which should alleviate the worse symptoms. William, still grumbling went off to find some from a machine down the corridor.

Bob, completely naked, sat on the edge of the bed holding his face. "Jesus, James, what am I going to do?" I sat on the bed with him, and as William came back with the ice, we put some into a napkin and applied it to Bob's cheek. William was not at all happy, mainly because he had obviously been excluded from the festivities but had been kept awake because of them. "I knew I shouldn't have let you use my room," he kept saying.

"It's a little late for that," I replied gently. "In any case, there is nothing else we can do tonight, I'll ask Liz to look in at Susie first thing in the morning, and in the meantime, I suggest we conjure up a story that will help the situation." I smiled confidently.

On my way back home, a little ruse was emerging in my mind. I could not let the wedding fail now we had all worked too hard to prepare for it. I climbed into bed at just after 3.30 in the morning, and Liz woke up as I did so, looking at the clock. I hastily told her what had happened and what I was going to do in the morning to try to get things back on track. Liz sniffed and turned over. I reluctantly turned the alarm on for 6 a.m. It was going to be a busy day.

I felt I had just about dozed off when the alarm went off. I had a shower and dressed quickly. Liz, always an early riser, got up too. I suggested that she go over to Susie in her room and that I would join her shortly. I then telephoned a doctor friend of mine, Jonathan Sethia, and told him what I needed. He was reluctant at first, but after offering him and his girlfriend a slap-up meal in the restaurant, he agreed.

Jonathan promised to be at my house by just after 8 a.m. I then rang William's room and after some considerable delay, Bob answered. I told him that both he and William should be at my house by eight. They both turned up just

35

before, Bob looking decidedly the worse for wear. He had the largest black eye. I have ever seen.

When Jonathan arrived, I told them what I wanted each one to do. William was a little reluctant at first but eventually after some bribery, he also agreed to the plan.

The way things were, we were not going to make too much money out of this wedding I thought to myself afterward.

Sending Bob and William off to the local hospital, with a note from Jonathan, we walked over to the hotel, found Susie's room, and knocked. Liz opened the door and whispered that Susie was in a bit of a state, as we walked in.

Susie was sitting cross-legged on the bed looking very red-eyed. She glowered at me. "Susie," I said before she could speak, 'I want you to meet Doctor Sethia, Doctor Jonathan Sethia..."

"Doctor..." Susie looked queryingly at Jonathan.

He smiled, his even white teeth contrasting his good Indian looks. "It's good to meet you Susie, and don't worry, I am sure that Bob is not badly hurt..."

Susie looked alarmed. "Badly hurt..."

"Yes," said Jonathan, sitting on the bed near her. "I have sent him off to hospital to have his cheek X-rayed, but I don't think he'll have any permanent damage..."

Susie frowned.

I took up the story, "You see Susie, last night it was William who took Bob back to his room because he was so drunk. He put Bob to bed, who by then was quite unconscious, and as he was still wide awake, he went out again, meeting up with..."

"But if what you say is true," said Susie, now looking decidedly unsure of herself, "why did I find that woman in bed with Bob?" I nodded. "You see after William had paid the girl off, he suggested she go, but apparently in the hope of getting two bites of the cherry, so to speak," I said smoothly, "she climbed into bed with Bob, not knowing he was completely out for the count. She had obviously just realised this when we got to the room," Jonathan nodded, and laughed "In my best medical opinion, Bob would have been in no fit state to do anything during the small hours of this morning, as his alcohol level was such, that he must have been totally incapable." I thought he lied beautifully.

"So, I don't blame you for reacting the way you did," I said, "and of course, Bob did get very drunk on the night before his wedding and..."

Susie let out a yelp of anguish, "oh poor Bob, what have I done..."

I held my hand up. "Don't worry, I don't think the hospital will keep him in, and I suggested to William, who took him up there early this morning, that I should take you up there." By 10 a.m., we had collected Bob from the hospital where at Jonathan's behest they had painted some purple disinfectant onto his face so that he looked even worse than he had done before. Susie was most repentant, particularly after William had made his 'confession,' which was to cost the Pub a lobster meal for two.

For my part, I felt I was justified in my little ruse, as after all Bob had been rather drunk at the time. In any case, almost anything was worth the saving of the wedding which was about to take place. By the end of the day, I was to wish that I had not interfered.

The wedding was scheduled for 3 p.m. that afternoon, so despite the morning shenanigans, we still had time to arrange everything.

Liz had brought in some staff early, and after duly delivering Bob, Susie, and William back to the hotel, I went back to the Pub to help. Liz had been busy making some cocktail snacks for the buffet afterward, leaving Yani and Gregory free to concentrate on the major items of food. As I took a tray of the cocktail bits into the cooler for her, I noticed Liz's full-length mink coat hung up in polythene wrapping amidst the various bits of food. I was surprised, as I had forgotten that she had brought it out from England, hen we first came out to the Caribbean. On returning to the kitchen, I asked why it was there.

"'Because the West Indian climate is not good for fur coats," she answered. "And besides, the moths would get it if I put it in a cupboard, and so the cooler is the best place for it, it was too expensive to be spoiled," She added.

"What about thieves," I ventured rather stupidly.

Liz looked at me. "And who, in the West Indies is going to run off with a fur coat?".

I smiled and nodded at her logic. Susie had persuaded the hotel manager to give her away, and they set off in a car well ahead of us. Liz joined Bob and me, and we gave him a good strong Bloody Mary, before driving over to the church. I had to smile, Bob really did look as though he had been in an argument with a ten-ton truck, and he received the appropriate sympathy from all concerned, sympathy which he certainly did not deserve.

Unfortunately, Bob was not the best of actors and instead of accepting Susie's obvious distress at what she had done, he had belaboured the point to the extent where Susie was becoming a bit suspicious. I told him to knock it off, and act normally.

The wedding service went off without a hitch and apart from Bob's face looking a little out of place on the wedding photograph the picture was duly taken.

Susie looked most attractive in a white lace dress, and one could not have believed the transformation since the early hours of the same morning.

After the service, the horse and trap were brought to the front of the church, with the photographs completed, and with a beaming vicar and all of us looking on, the bride and groom climbed in. Bob took the reins from the handlers, and he confidently whipped them down on the horse's flank. Now in normal circumstances, a trained horse would have cantered off at a reasonable pace. The problem as I suspected later was that the horse used for the day, was one that had not even been in a trap before, and the confines of the two shafts plus Bob's over-enthusiastic thrashing of the reins was more than the poor animal was prepared to accept without a show of rebellion.

There was a sudden jerk, throwing Bob and Susie backward against their seat and the horse simply bolted out of the churchyard, turning left on one wheel at the main road in the manner of a formula one-race car, and then disappearing from our sight. A taxi that had been driving along the road had to swerve violently to miss the sudden appearance of the couple, and the driver who had just bought himself a large ice cream from the local post office ended up with the lot up his nose. When I first saw him, I thought he had been shaving while driving.

I realised that at the speed the trap was going, it would not take long for some disaster to happen, and as the handler ran after the disappearing trio, I grabbed Liz, and we rushed to get in the van.

Quickly starting it, we drove carefully through the throng of people who were headed for the entrance, no doubt expecting to see an upside-down trap in the middle of the road. Surprisingly, as we turned left, we could see nothing but the empty road, apart from the enraged taxi driver, and various people walking towards us on the roadside all with their heads pointed the other way at a cloud of dust.

We continued cautiously to the crossroads, where we would normally have turned right to get back to the Pub, but we could clearly see the dust cloud had gone straight on across the major road. I silently thanked God that nothing had been coming the other way. The road opposite the one we were on, was not really a road at all, more a mud trail and it was quite wet after the recent rains. We knew the riding school had its headquarters about half a mile down the track, so we crossed over and negotiated the stones and potholes on the lane we now found ourselves in. It was a quarter of a mile further on when we came to the sorry-looking couple.

The wheel had come off the left-hand side of the trap, and occupants and the trap had tipped over into the sewer drain. Bob had hurt his arm and could not move it properly, but Susie seemed fine, except that her wedding dress was torn and soiled and they both smelled like sewer rats. The horse had completely disappeared.

We helped them both into the van and managed to turn it around in the small space just as the handler caught us up. He appeared intent on claiming damages from poor Bob, but I ignored him and put my foot down hard on the accelerator, and when I looked in my rear-view mirror, I was pleased to see that our rear wheels had sprayed wet mud all over the unreasonable handler.

When we got back to the Pub, Liz took Susie back to the hotel to change, and I had Bob taken to the hospital, this time for a genuine problem to have his arm checked.

Liz arrived back at the Pub with Susie before Bob returned, and I told them both that I had just telephoned the hospital, and they confirmed that they had found a cracked bone in his arm. Whether they had or not it was the general practice to put any suspect limb into plaster, as this gave all the student nurses much-needed training in the art of treating broken limbs. The fact that they had someone who would also pay for this was a bonus.

Although a bit shaken at first. Susie suggested we not wait for Bob, and start the buffet and as the musicians arrived, we all soon started to dance. As time went on, I noticed from time to time that Susie was getting rather inebriated, but I passed it off as being natural in the circumstances. After all, I told myself, she had had rather an unusual day. The last time I noticed her before Bob returned, was that she was dancing a rather slow piece with Yani. She seemed to be clinging to him a bit more than I would have expected.

It must have been about twenty minutes later that Bob arrived back, now with his right arm in plaster and in a sling. It was dark outside, and the party was going full stretch in the Yachtsman's bar. I looked around for Susie but could not see her. I spied Liz and extracted her from some hopeful St Lucian male who thought he had captured his partner for the night.

"Have you seen Susie?" She shook her head. "No, perhaps she's in the lavatory?"

I shook my head, "No, I've checked, both ladies and gents are currently empty. I hope she's all right," I added, Susie had been drinking rather a lot and we were always a little worried when guests drank heavily because it would be very easy to go outside on the veranda for a breath of fresh air and drop into the lagoon, without anyone noticing. I went outside and looked down towards the water which was lit by the lights from the Pub. We couldn't see anything, which was somewhat of a relief.

"Oh, wait a minute," I said suddenly, "I remember seeing Susie and Yani heading for the kitchen..." I sighed with relief. "Yani is probably showing her the kitchens," I said.

Liz frowned. I told I would go and check, which I did, but as I walked into the kitchen there was the usual bustle of waitresses coming in and out, and Gregory was busy on preparing some fish dishes. "Have you seen chef?" I asked him.

He did not look at me. "No sir,"

"Gregory," I growled...

Just then Sylvia came in. "Have you seen Chef, Sylvia?" She looked at me in amusement, "I tink he be in de cooler," she grinned, as she grabbed the fish dish from Gregory, and disappeared in a fit of giggles into the restaurant.

"In the cooler?" I repeated aloud. Puzzled I walked over opened the heavy door and walked in closing it behind me. I heard a muffled sound ahead and switched the light on. I could not believe my eyes.

Susie was laid backward over several boxes, her skirt around her waist, with her feet on the floor and her arms tightly around Yani. Yani was wearing Liz's fur coat and was on top of Susie. It did not take more than a second for me to realise precisely what was going on.

"You can't do that in here," I yelped at Yani.

He turned his head and grinned, the movement in the lower part of his body continuing to be in motion without a break in rhythm. "I can and I am." He said turning his attention back to a giggling Susie who had taken not the slightest interest in me.

I was furious, stepping forward and tearing Liz's fur coat off his back. Yani was naked apart from socks and shoes. "Well, if you can, then you can bloody well continue without fur," I snapped as I turned to leave, I saw Yani's clothes in a heap on the floor, and I scooped them up and went out followed by a yell from Yani.

I placed his clothes on a kitchen counter and went to find Liz.

"What on earth are you doing with my coat?" She asked when she saw me.

I told her.

"God that bloody man, I'll..." Liz clenched her fists.

"Well, I shouldn't worry, I think I might have cooled his ardour somewhat."

I was told by a giggling Sylvia that Yani had not stayed very long in the cooler and had appeared with a cardboard box around his nether quarters, and the rest of him displaying rather large goose pimples. Susie had come out and gone straight over to Bob. The last thing we saw of them that night was both in an embrace as they wandered aimlessly around the dance floor.

The next day, Susie acted as though nothing had happened, and they continued their honeymoon, leaving for England a week later.

"I think we'll give weddings a miss for a while," I said after they had left the island. We were to be involved with two more, but they went relatively smoothly, thank goodness.

It was some years later that we were to call on Susie and Bob who by then lived in Tunbridge Wells in Kent. They were very proper and responsible. They had two children and Bob was a respected member of Rotary. We had the feeling that they were uncomfortable with our visit, as our presence, no doubt brought back memories that did not quite suit their present environment.

THE SPY THAT WASN'T

CHAPTER
4

"We are all spies, but the clever ones.
get paid."

This is a true story.

At the age of 25, I secured a management job in Nigeria with a company called the British West African Corporation. Because the West Coast of Africa was not high on the list of where people wished to work, (known as the 'arm pit' of Africa) the responsibility one received was far above one's capability and experience, as was the pay and conditions.

There was a drawback in that as a young married man, I had to leave my wife, Elizabeth, and children in the UK for three months before they could join me. I was delayed in being sent out there due to a military coup where the elected President Nnamdi Azikiwe was deposed and Prime Minister Abubakar Balewa, formerly a school teacher was assassinated, the government was taken over by Major General Ironsi. Once the 'dust' had settled, I flew out to take up my management position.

This was the start of a general unrest in Nigeria, as Abubakar was a Politician attached to the Hausa in the Muslim north, (by far the most populous tribe). His assassination by an Igbo from the South East meant trouble. I had only been in Nigeria for a short time having welcomed my family joining me, when General Ironsi was in turn assassinated and government control was taken over by General Gowan, from the Tiv tribe allied to the Hausa. It became obvious that the Igbo would rebel, which they did by seceding from the union, naming the new state Biafra.

The problems came thick and fast as Biafra held all the country's oil reserves. My first position was in a town called Port Harcourt, the principal oil town in Nigeria, where we also had a large factory assembling Land Rovers and trucks. Subsequently, I was promoted to open a new branch of the company in Onitsha in the northwest of Biafra which, because of the river Niger, was a strategic military outpost. This was due to it being host to the only bridge between the Federal and Biafran forces. This bridge was 1.4 miles in length. The Niger is the third largest river in Africa with a length of 2,600 miles. The source of the river is in the Guinea highlands north of Sierra Leone and thus it splits Nigeria, north to south, and as a result, both sides were protected by substantial military assets.

Because the situation was a proxy war between on one side the British and Americans, supporting the Federal forces, and the Biafrans supported by the French, we were not the flavour of the day where we were situated. The opening unrest triggered riot squads looking for Hausa servants, which fortunately we had none. We did have a letter from one ex-servant threatening Elizabeth's life, but he was an Igbo.

One memorable instance, however, was when we were travelling downtown in our car with the children, we were trapped in a traffic jam caused by a riot. There were people by the roadside who had their heads removed amid screaming individuals banging on our car with sticks and machetes. At the time we were more concerned with ensuring our children did not see the blood and gore at the side of the road, than worrying about our personal safety.

The second instance came when I was in my office, on the first floor of our commercial building on the main street of the town. It became obvious there was another much larger riot, but in this case, the police were trying to quell it by firing tear gas. I got my employees to come into my office and we locked the door pending the police dealing with the unrest. What I had forgotten, was my air conditioning was going full blast, the day being particularly hot. This was made

44

worse by the number of people now in the same room. If I had thought about it, I would have realised that air conditioners draw the air from outside, and in this case, it did so with some efficiency, including the tear gas, with the most unpleasant results. We had no choice but to flee outside, and I eventually arrived home with streaming tears.

The next weekend, we decided to motor to the capital Enugu to buy European food, which was no longer available in Onitsha. Despite various police and army checkpoints, we had an uneventful drive, arriving at our branch there after about 3 hours. We were in Elizabeth's car, which was a Sunbeam Alpine sports car. As we neared Enugu, I detected a problem with the gearbox, so, on arrival I handed the car to our service department to see what the problem was. Elizabeth and the children went shopping, while I spent some time taking photographs of mainly agricultural equipment that had just arrived from the south. On my return to the branch, I was warned by the English manager that our car had been seized by the police and 2 of our African mechanics, who were checking it out on the road, had been thrown into jail. He then showed me a copy of an arrest warrant which stated that I was wanted as a British Spy. Our senior management assumed that the Biafran government was trying to compromise the company since we made Land Rovers and trucks for the Nigerian Army, our factory being in Port Harcourt, situated in Biafra.

I was whisked away with my wife and children to the local manager's house, which fortunately was within a large compound at the end of a long drive. We all had to sleep in the drawing room with strict orders to dive out of the back door into the jungle behind, should anyone approach the villa. We didn't sleep easily, and the thought of trying to camp out in a snake-invested environment was not very palatable. Later the next morning, we were told the matter had been partly resolved and we should travel back to Onitsha ASAP. Unfortunately, the car was by then a wreck, as the security goons had completely torn out all the upholstery, presumably in their quest for microfilm.

We borrowed a company Land Rover to return, and at the last army checkpoint, one of the soldiers inadvertently

45

pointed his submachine gun at our children in the back. An enraged Elizabeth immediately stepped out of the vehicle and attacked the unfortunate soldier with a bag of apples. I thought our end had come...

Fortunately, the other 10 soldiers thought it was funny, particularly as the offender crouched down to avoid Elizabeth's apple onslaught. He was not laughing, however, and we only breathed a sigh of relief when we turned a corner further up the road out of sight.

I had been designated by the British Embassy as one of the people to help evacuate Europeans in the event of further troubles and we placed 2 further Land Rover estates in our large garage underneath the house, which contained food and medical supplies.

It was not to be, as shortly after returning to Onitsha, I became very ill from Hepatitis A, a virus caught from infected water. (More probably ice served in the gin and tonics at the European clubhouse). Because of the lack of medicines at the time, it didn't look as though I would survive. My illness worsened because I refused to stay in the local Borromeo hospital due to the local riots. Thankfully however, the sister doctor (it was a Catholic hospital) managed to smuggle some medication across the border from West Germany, which helped my condition, but I was told by the doctors that I had to be got back to the UK ASAP.

We had a friend who managed a garage owned by the John Holt organisation in Onitsha, and as he was an ex-Major in the old British Nigerian Army, he offered the services of a man who worked for him and who had been his Nigerian Sergeant Major. He kindly agreed to drive us to Benin in the mid-southwest.

As we had no other way of getting out, we thankfully agreed, and it was decided we should set off about 20.00 hours, as to go later would arouse suspicions.

We got through the army checkpoint on the Biafran side of the bridge, but when stopped at the other side, we were greeted by some very unfriendly Federal soldiers. The Sergeant Major explained that I was ill and that he was evacuating me and my family, but they were not sympathetic, ordering us all out of the car. The children started crying and the soldiers started to rough up the Sergeant Major. I stepped forward to explain, and one of the goons stuck a submachine gun at my stomach. It was then that an officer walked over and asked what was going on, and he spied the Sergeant Major. It was lucky for us that they knew each other, and they shook hands, the officer telling his men to leave us alone and that we could go.

It took us a further 3 hours to reach Benin, where we were dropped off at the local rest house. The next morning, we caught a plane to Lagos, and from there to the United Kingdom. We learned later that the next plane taking off from Benin to Lagos was hijacked back to Enugu in Biafra. I also learned later that the person giving permission for me to leave Enugu had himself been arrested.

When we arrived back in the UK, we had a message from the company that our house in Onitsha had been bombed by the Federal forces, (It was never confirmed that it was the Federal forces that carried out the bombing) and everything destroyed, including my car, a Rover 3 litre, the Land Rovers under our house and all our personal effects. Three weeks later we had a letter from a depositary in Chatham where we had put our UK furniture into the store. It said that they had experienced a devastating fire, and all our furniture had been destroyed. At least we took comfort in that we were at least insured for that, but we never received anything for the goods destroyed in Onitsha nor for Elizabeth's car left in Enugu.

We were never able to go back to Nigeria, as all expatriates were evacuated by the British Navy some weeks after we had left. I spent six months recovering, spending some time in the hospital for tropical diseases in London, before obtaining a job running a company in Scotland.

A year later we returned to West Africa, this time to Ghana where I was given the job as the chief executive of a company owned by John Holt's of Liverpool. This was a shipping company that had been deeply involved in the kidnapping of three German boats from Fernando Po in West Africa during World War 2. (Called Operation Postmaster).

47

Holt's had motor distribution, a factory building Chrysler trucks in Takoradi, Ashanti Goldfields in Kumasi, and Peto breweries. It also hosted a 'political' operation run by a retired senior MI6 man who had been attached to the British Embassy in Moscow, and an ex-Naval Commander. So, the name 'spy' stuck, mainly because of my association with companies and people who were connected to the secret world. I did then become involved in various military matters, one organising the trial of the British Hovercraft Corporation (I still have the film of that) who sent a military version out to Ghana, and the sale of an ex-navy destroyer belonging to President Nkrumah who had recently been assassinated. It was sold to the Republic of Ireland. I was also friendly with other British agents who worked out of the Embassy in Accra. They were connected to a special branch, which meant they were embedded in various rural areas, sometimes virtually living in mud huts.

It may be wondered why an Englishman working for a large business at senior level, particularly if it is selling British goods anywhere in the world, is of interest to MI6 and other agencies. It's obvious really, as it enables the political men, as they are called in the British Embassies, to keep his or her ears to the ground. In Ghana, I was second in command of the John Holt operation there, so despite my age, I was a senior manager and director. Several of the embassy staff became firm friends, and we met regularly to play the game of Diplomacy. When we moved to Jamaica, I was contacted by the 'political man' there, and we became good friends with him and his wife. He was subsequently promoted back to the UK, and we continued our association when we also moved back to the UK.

When we returned to the Caribbean, I became much more involved, as my business partner, a senior lawyer also worked with the CIA, and was chairman of Saint Lucia Airways, an operation owned by the spy agency. As a result, and because I had developed a very accurate method of processing data, I was asked to set up an operation near Washington DC to carry out work for them.

Definition of a Spy:

48

1. One who secretly collects information concerning the enemies of a government or group.

2. One who secretly collects information for a business about one or more of its competitors.

3. One who secretly keeps watch on another or others.

I could be accused of all three of the above. Certainly, I am aware of certain things not designed for public knowledge, and I have used my interpretation of certain instances in my series of books, published under the heading of 'Behind the News' but they are fiction largely based on fact. Spies are normally paid for the specific job of intelligence gathering. I have never been paid for that specific type of work, so, having said that, I was never a spy.

CHAPTER
5

"Or does democracy threaten.
digitisation?"

This is a factual story discussed in the fictional book 'the Shanghai Incident' regarding China and Russia.

Before discussing digitisation, I need to discuss codes and cyphers, as they are essential to the proliferation of the digital age to ensure our data is safe and only available to those who should receive it.

A cypher is a method of sending a plain text in code that is unintelligible to anyone but the recipient.

We know that Julius Caesar used cyphers to communicate between his legions, they were simple but effective at that time. The problem with a cypher is that if someone other than the recipient can break it, it is no longer any use.

Mary Queen of Scots used a cypher when communicating with members of the Babington plot, the problem was the cypher was given to her by a trusted friend, who was working for the enemy, the enemy being Walsingham our first real spymaster. It cost her life. The point here is if you are using a cypher; make sure you know where it comes from.

As time went on, the search for a safer cypher was important, as diplomatic secret reports needed to be passed between countries. Of course, we talk about secrecy, but nothing is really secret once more than one person has the same knowledge, but the idea is to ensure that only the people who should have the information, receive it, it being gibberish to others who should not.

The modern innovation for cyphers came from a Frenchman named Blaise de Vigenère who developed a table of 26 letters by 26 letters which enabled the use of 'keys'. This prevented a code breaker from finding similarities in the cypher text. A key incidentally could be a simple word. However, nowadays keys are often as long as the message making decryption much more difficult.

The Vigenère system was eventually compromised (broken), and the most publicised result was the breaking of the Zimmerman telegram by the British during World War 1, which brought the Americans into the war. In fact, the breaking of the cypher was only one of the machinations the British went through to ensure there was no suspicion that it was they who had deciphered it. It is possible that if Zimmerman himself had not confirmed that he had sent it, the telegram would not have had the same impact. The lesson here for anyone in the secrets business is, if you do not have to admit anything, keep quiet or deny it.

For those that don't know the Zimmerman story, it was sent to the President of Mexico by the German Foreign Office offering to support Mexico in cash and supplies to invade the USA and annex Texas, New Mexico, and Arizona.

The next major innovation was invented by a German named Arthur Scherbius, and this is where we enter the machine age in cryptology. At first, the Germans were not interested in this machine which today we call the enigma, but the Poles were, and for this we were fortunate, but this is not relevant to this story.

After the Second World War, commercial companies were as keen as countries to have an unbreakable cypher that could be used by anyone who wanted to encrypt their data or financial transactions. This became critical when digitisation became available to the masses, which was in 1981 when the personal computer started to be freely available.

What was required was a method whereby the recipient did not need to hold the key, and this is where RSA came into being. RSA was invented by three Americans called Rivest, Shamir, and Adleman who devised a method of being able to send a privately encrypted message, with the person at the other end being able to use a public key to decrypt it or vice versa. The basis of the system is the use of prime numbers. For those of you who want to know exactly how it works, go to the following link: (doctrina.org/How-RSA-Works-With-Examples.html).

They became multi-millionaires as a result, but a British man, Clifford Cocks, who invented a similar process much earlier was not allowed to publish or patent his invention due the fact that he worked for GCHQ.

The problem with cypher systems is that they are invented by ingenious people, but in all cases so far, there have been just as clever people who have been able to break the cyphers. A cypher developed between just two people using what is called a one-time pad cypher is still almost impossible to break, but it's unusable once one needs to communicate with more than one person, and certainly unusable in commercial or government terms.

Unfortunately, RSA is now compromised, meaning that it is no longer safe. Indeed, there is already a method suggesting how it may be broken posted on the web, Google: "RSA compromised" if you're interested.

Of course, you don't get hordes of people shouting about it, as the longer the majority are not aware a cypher can be broken, the more those who wish to read encrypted messages can continue to do so. It is worrying though as all our financial transactions rely on RSA or derivatives such as PGP (Plenty Good Privacy) of this system.

So, if the present cypher system can be broken, where do we go from here? In my book 'The Shanghai Incident', I have suggested a method using WW2 technology along with lasers, but it would only be of use for governments and would not work with the current technology for commercial use. This novel also deals with the destruction of the Chinese hacking centre in the Pudong area of Shanghai.

Now to look at why encryption is so important aside from secret communications. PLCs and PCMs (programmable logic controllers and power control modules) are mini-industrial computers built into almost all industrial machinery to control specific processes such as flight controls on an aeroplane, hospitals, dams, sewerage works, street lights, traffic lights, trains, vehicles of all types, (built after 1983), ships, generating stations, gas supplies, communications, nuclear power stations and many other things we take for granted.

Originally, PLCs were built into machinery to make it more efficient and to enable diagnostics to be carried out by skilled operatives. Some of the original PLC's codes were not even encrypted. With the advent of the internet, it was decided that instead of paying lots of maintenance teams, all these mini-computers in static installations should be linked to the worldwide web, thus saving large sums of money. It was a great idea, except by doing so, they are now all susceptible to hacking.

When you consider hacking, the thought is that a piece of machinery will simply be shut down, secrets read or data changed, but there is a greater danger. When Iran was trying to build an atomic bomb, they had thousands of centrifuges linked to the internet. The Americans broke in and rather than close them down, they instructed the internal PLCs to increase the speeds that exceeded the maker's safety barriers and thus they self-destructed. When the Iranians realised what was happening, they moved what was left underground and linked them together on their own circuit. A Mossad employee simply infected the system by using a flash drive. The program devised by the CIA was called Stuxnet. It took the Iranians about two years to recover. The message here is never to allow anyone to put a flash drive into your computer as it could carry a virus, sometimes unbeknown to the owner of the flash drive.

Now, most equipment is encrypted and thus more difficult to break into, but once hacked, a simple instruction from a computer on the internet can cause havoc. Flash drives the size of a small coin can devastate a huge factory, and remember, a worm or virus introduced can destroy equipment instead of just shutting it down. Imagine a terrorist hacking into a train, disabling the braking system, and increasing the speed to unacceptable levels.

The danger is about to become even greater. To decrypt a complicated cypher can take time, and in theory, in some scenarios, it could take a thousand years even using supercomputers. A normal PC can deal with about 65 thousand bits per second, but now we have the advent of the Quantum computer. A 50-qubit computer would be able to deal with 1,125 quadrillion bits per second. (A billion, billion). This means that it could decrypt any cypher or code in a split second. Because of the extraordinary power of these new machines that rely on quantum physics, it is almost certain that machines have been built with considerably more qubits than the 20 already admitted, but no country wishes to publicise the fact that they have such power. In fact, Google has just announced that they have produced a Quantum computer that answered a question that a supercomputer would take ten thousand years to answer. It took just three seconds. Can you imagine if unregulated companies like Google can harness such power, where does that leave us?

This is the future; nothing will be safe. Even now, an expert with a laptop can break into any car made after 1983 and take control of it from outside by entering the vehicle's computer diagnostic system. The reason laptops were prevented from being taken into the cabin on airline flights, was due to the concern that they could be used to take control of an aircraft. We already know that hackers have been able to break into the US military systems, supposedly with the best computer defences in the world. Now we are handing the manufacturing of 5G phones to the Chinese, thus allowing them to create 'back-doors' which will enable them to harvest our data.

The thought is that if you are not guilty of anything, it doesn't matter who reads your data or listens in to your telephone calls, but it will if your bank account is cleared out, your identity is stolen, your medical records are changed, or scammers use your data to damage your reputation or steal money from you in other ways other than through your bank.

In the future, wars could effectively be won or lost within 24 hours, the winner being the country that has the fastest computer technology and the best defensive measures. Of course, defences will have to be built to counteract this digital threat; the best defence is for the recipient to send an electronic 'bomb' back to where the hacker is located and destroy the equipment used, (and maybe the hacker too) but we do not yet have this capability and indeed such an act may be too late anyway.

The other danger of those owning quantum computers is the ability to capture data from all digitised sources including encrypted social media and to use algorithms to create detailed preferences. Hugely useful for manipulating voters in national elections. The same data can be used to create 'fake news', which can create doubts about a politician, party, or even another country.

We should not underestimate Corbyn. Putin almost certainly managed to ensure the Trump campaign won in the

USA. We must assume he will do the same here. Imagine, if he was successful in helping to get the current socialist party elected with a majority, he would have achieved a situation where the UK would withdraw from NATO, reduce our defence spending, and destroy our nuclear deterrent. Quite a prize.

Welcome to the new world!

CRETE - A LIFE EXPERIENCE

CHAPTER
6

"things I know, is that I know nothing. This is the source of my wisdom." - Socrates

This story is based on my experience, living on the island for four years.

Crete is the largest and southernmost of 6,000 Greek islands of which only 181 are inhabited. Its climate is temperate, but it can get quite cold in the winter. Last year we even had snow! It is 160 miles long, between 10 and 37 miles wide, and about 100 miles by sea from Athens in the North and a similar distance from the North African coastline in the South. It is mostly mountainous in the centre and the west and the bulk of the population of 600,000 live in the Northern towns. The main tourist area is in the East, but the West claims to be a cultural area. The South side of the island is sparsely populated but has several ancient monasteries and walkable gorges. The Samarian Gorge is one of the longest in Europe, I know, we walked it, PHEW. It is not recommended unless you are very fit.

Crete is thought to have had the oldest civilisation recorded in Europe dated from 2,600 BC to 1,700 BC. Like Troy, the Minoan civilisation was considered a myth, but this became a reality when an Englishman called Sir Arthur Evans discovered the ruins of King Minos's palace at Knossos. This is indeed a site to see as it originally had 1,400 rooms on five floors, running water, and proper sewerage.

Interestingly the palace was not fortified, suggesting that the Minoans had few enemies. They were basically traders and as a result, had a large navy. There are other Minoan palaces that have now been excavated including the summer palace at Phaistos in the south, but Knossos is where the Minotaur was supposed to live in the Labyrinth under the palace.

The Minoans suffered a cataclysmic occurrence around 1,450 BC when the surface of the island was destroyed by fire. This was due to the devastating explosion of the island volcano under Santorini, 30 miles north of Crete. Santorini had a huge underground volcano like the one in Yellowstone Park in the USA and Kick 'em, Jenny, in the lower Caribbean. This erupted and blew itself and most of the island of Santorini to pieces. The explosion was so large, that it has been suggested it was up to 10 times greater than that of Krakatoa, the largest volcanic explosion in our own recorded history, which was on an Indonesian island in 1883. The explosion emanating from the Santorini volcano would have been equal to 100 hydrogen bombs, throwing huge rocks and hot ash onto Crete. Due to the Minoans' practice of storing olive oil in large containers, it decimated all the dwellings there. What was left was destroyed by the subsequent massive tsunami that not only affected Crete but all parts of the Mediterranean. This is probably why no human remains have been found on Crete from that era. The people who escaped from Crete populated the countries around the Eastern Mediterranean, and the later Pharaohs including the well-documented Queen of Egypt, Cleopatra were reputed to be descended from the Minoan civilisation.

Recently the BBC did a documentary suggesting that the explosion of Santorini could have been connected to the crossing of the Israelites from Egypt. They argued forcibly that they did not cross the Red Sea, but the reed salt lakes in the north, where the tsunami would have drawn all the water out of the area allowing the Israelites to cross over to Sinai, but by the time the Pharaoh's army reached the spot, the waters would have closed the gap, and in such a case, I suppose the church would argue that it was God who created the explosion of the volcano rather than the actual parting of the sea. One cannot but wonder whether this was also the 'flood' of Noah's Ark, and the disappearance of Atlantis, as the underwater remains of Santorini coincide with Plato's description of the lost city.

Crete has been populated by humans since around 6,000 BC and subsequently, it was occupied by the Minoans, Mycenaeans, Dorian Greeks, Pirates, Romans, Byzantium, Venetians, Turks and eventually it became part of Greece in 1913 thanks to Britain wresting control of the island from the Turks. In May 1941, the Germans occupied Crete until 1945. At the end of the war, they refused to surrender to the Greeks because they knew that due to the appalling atrocities they had carried out against the Cretans, they would all be killed by the local population, so the British had to fly in troops to take their surrender.

World War 2 at this stage it is worth mentioning how the German invasion of Crete may have had a positive disproportionate effect on the European conflict. Mussolini stupidly invaded Greece through Albania, looking for an easy victory. It didn't work as planned and the Greeks hit back with a force that suggested Italy could be defeated. Britain entered the fray by sending troops from North Africa to support Greece. Hitler, seeing such an intervention could put the important Romanian oil fields in jeopardy from the British air force, sent in his Panzer Divisions already earmarked for the Russian invasion. The result was a humiliating defeat for the British who were evacuated to Crete by courtesy of the British navy, leaving most of their equipment on the Greek mainland.

Crete had no infrastructure to accept a sudden influx of over 30,000 troops and the soldiers, most without arms, had to look after themselves, sleeping in the open on makeshift beds without cover within the olive groves that permeate the island. Fortunately, the weather was warm as it was in May 1941.

Enter General Student who was a senior Luftwaffe Officer in charge of the highly trained German parachute battalion. He was keen to utilise this force and supported by his boss, Reich Marshall Goering, he persuaded Hitler to allow an invasion of Crete to threaten the Suez Canal while at the same time preventing the British army from reinforcing North Africa with the troops saved from Greece.

The details of the emerging plan were decrypted by Bletchley Park (known as ULTRA) and Churchill decided to block the invasion, putting an army General in charge of organising a defence. One of Churchill's failures was he was not always good at picking the right men to do the job. He greatly admired those that had shown bravery under fire and so he appointed a British-born New Zealand General called Bernard Freyberg VC to command. Brave men do not always make good Generals, however.

Freyberg set about trying to organise the polyglot of Australian, New Zealand, and British soldiers on the island, but he was the only person who was cleared for ULTRA, and while he knew exactly when the Germans would arrive, he kept that secret from his subordinate generals, most of whom were considerably more proficient than him. An example of Freyberg's organisational abilities was exposed when General Wavell asked what equipment he would like to have sent over from North Africa. Freyberg gave a list of armaments including tanks but excluded wireless sets of which there were virtually none on Crete.

Because of its mountainous topography, Crete is wholly unsuitable for tank warfare and those that were sent were soon out of action. It was the absence of the defenders not being able to communicate that was critical however, and this was the main cause for the failure of the British being able to hold the island. Nevertheless, when the attack came over 4,000 German paratroopers were slaughtered as they landed, which prohibited the use of the German parachute Battalion being used again during the war.

The Germans also sent several thousand reinforcements from southern Greece by barge and the British navy intercepted all but one. It was expensive with the loss of 10 warships out of thirty-one with 19 damaged. The Royal Navy casualty list was 2,295 killed or missing, Mountbatten's HMS Kelly being one of those lost. This was because Germany had overwhelming air power in the region. Nevertheless, an estimated 13,000 highly trained German mountain troops perished in the sea. The British learned that the barges could be overturned simply by the wash of a destroyer, which perhaps suggests that if Hitler had invaded Britain with his Operation Sea Lion, in a sea quite different from the Mediterranean, our forty destroyers available in the channel area against Germany's two, would have decimated his army, even had he gained air supremacy over the Royal Air Force.

So, what else was fundamental in the invasion of Greece and Crete? Hitler seriously delayed the Russian invasion by several weeks, so it was the 22nd of June before Operation Barbarossa was launched. This meant that victory could not be achieved before the fierce Russian winter, thus catching the German troops without adequate clothing or proper equipment protection. They never really recovered from this time-lapse and did not take a strategic advantage from the capture of Crete, and toward the end of the war, it proved to be a step too far as he didn't have the resources to invade Russia and the Suez Canal.

During the siege of Leningrad which ended in January 1944, Goering boasted that he would be able to supply the German troops pending a breakout but forgot that a very high percentage of his transport planes had been destroyed in the Crete invasion, thus forcing an eventual humiliating German surrender to the Russians.

On the other side of the coin, when British and Polish parachutists were dropped near Arnhem in Holland in 1944, the German General in charge of the region was General Student, the one man in the German military who understood the parachute regiment and how they would operate.

GREEK MYTHOLOGY CONNECTED TO CRETE

The original ruler of the gods was Uranus who was overthrown by his youngest son Kronos, (not to be confused with Cronos, the god of time) who, to prevent the same thing from happening to himself ate his first five children at birth. When Rhea his wife was pregnant with her sixth child, she took refuge in a Cretan cave where she gave birth to Zeus. She presented Kronos with a rock wrapped in a blanket which he duly ate. Zeus was brought up in the cave and was fed on milk from the goat-nymph Amalthea. Having grown to manhood on Crete, Zeus declared war on Kronos and the Titans, a war which lasted ten years and left him the supreme ruler of the gods on Mount Olympus. King Minos was the son of Zeus. The story goes on but gets far more complicated as Zeus then made Kronos regurgitate the five siblings he had eaten - A fascinating story.

BEQUIA

CHAPTER
7

"The problem with sailing in
the Caribbean is meeting a French boat".

---
*This is a part of an early chapter in Sailing on Silver and
is based on fact.*

We had now been in the Caribbean for 12 days, and so
we decided to take the next step in our journey south. About
three hours sail from Bequia, almost due east, is the island of
Mustique which means Mosquito in French. Liz thought it
would be a good idea to stop off there for at least a day, before
going down to the Grenadines proper. After lunch, everyone
felt lethargic. The stay in Bequia had been uneventful and
we'd been lulled into a feeling of peaceful euphoria, a state
that was about to be rudely shattered. We all turned in early.
Although the next day's sail wasn't a long one, I was
beginning to realise that the earlier one does things on a
boat, the more time there is to cope with disasters.

Suddenly, I was woken by a large bang on the side of
Shady Lady. In a container made of fibreglass, which was
what Shady Lady effectively was, any sound however slight
reverberates and amplifies. This sounded as though
something large and heavy had hit the boat hard. I went into
a cold sweat. My immediate thought was that the anchor had
come free, and we were on the rocks.

Unfortunately, I still hadn't learned that one
shouldn't move too quickly on a boat, particularly just after
waking. When we had gone to bed, the hatch to our cabin

roof had been open. I naturally expected that it still was. In my haste to stick my head through to discover the cause of the bang, I found out that it was closed.

"Ooooww," I shouted, as my head made contact with the Plexiglas, and I was catapulted straight back towards the berth. "F***, F***, F***," I hissed, as I nursed the already painful and tender parts of my body still not recovered from previous ill use.

Liz was now fully awake.

"Do you mind NOT using four-letter words," Liz's Methodist upbringing came to the fore.

"Why the hell did you close the hatch?"

"Because it started to rain, anyway what on earth are you doing? It's after midnight," Liz was looking at her luminous clock by the side of her berth.

"Didn't you hear the bang?" I asked.

She hadn't.

I heard someone moving on the deck above us and I immediately thought of the murdered skipper in Cumberland Bay. Only the previous day, we'd also heard a similar story of an unfortunate Canadian knifed and killed while asleep in his yacht over in Friendship Bay. Friendship is the bay on the south end of Bequia. I swallowed hard, and gently opened the hatch. It was Anne. She was already up and apparently having an urgent conversation with someone.

I hastily put on some shorts, and carefully negotiated the cabin entrance, climbed onto the aft deck, and quickly established what had happened. A French boat had come in late and anchored too near to Shady Lady. As their vessel was made of concrete and therefore much heavier than Shady Lady, it didn't swing in the wind as quickly as the fibreglass vessel, which is why it had made contact. It was an immediate relief to me to find that the anchor hadn't moved but it became clear that Anne was having a very acrimonious exchange with someone on the offending boat.

"Degagez, degagez," (Push Off).

The small man on the French yacht was gesticulating wildly.

"And you, fuck off, you little creep, we were here first,"

shouted Anne. "I wonder where she learned that language," I muttered to Liz, who had just joined me on deck.

The Frenchman let off a string of verbal abuse in return.

"He'd look rather like a stick insect if he didn't have that mop of dark hair," whispered.

Anne was in her element. While she didn't comprehend the content of the Frenchman's speech, the way he delivered it was crystal clear. She snarled something that questioned the Frenchman's lineage and put a fender down between the two boats. The Frenchman became even more agitated. Liz noticed that three small children a youngish woman, whom she assumed was the mother and, an older woman, who appeared to be Grandma, arrived on the deck of the other boat. Their yacht started to close with Shady Lady again, and the Frenchman became quite hysterical, jumping up and down on the deck, shaking his fist. Another stream of French came across, and my confrontational ire was now up. I went and stood by Anne to give verbal support. By this time, the young woman and Grandma had joined in, the young woman gesticulating wildly. The noise was such that various disturbed yachtsmen were switching on cabin lights around the area. Liz came up behind me.

"For God's sake, let's move," said Liz. "It doesn't matter who's right and who's wrong, the whole bay will be awake if this goes on," I was about to give an answer when Anne turned around to Liz momentarily suspending the exchange of good plain English invective.

"Not bloody likely," she growled. "Do you know what he just called me?" Before she'd a chance to tell, Liz the Frenchman made his big mistake. He'd picked up a long boat hook off his deck and was prodding it into the side of Shady Lady. His idea was to push the boats further apart but at the expense of Shady Lady's freeboard. We heard a scrape on the side of the yacht and Anne moved with unfamiliar speed. She grabbed the end of the hook and pulled. Unfortunately, the Frenchman caught completely off balance didn't let go. He was standing between a gap on the surrounding wire structure that most boats have, to stop people from falling off the deck and he had been bending forward slightly. For a split second, he teetered on the brink, with a comical expression on his face and then he went overboard with a loud splash. The young woman, who had seen what was going to happen, tried to catch him, and only just managed to stop falling in too. Anne dropped the boat hook just as the Frenchman was surfacing, and there was a howl, as it caught him squarely on the top of his head. Anne's honour was satisfied, as there appeared to be no more abuse to exchange, leaving what she clearly thought was the 'mopping up' to those less skilled in the art of international diplomacy.

She returned to her cabin, grumbling, and growling as she went, missing seeing the Frenchman's toupee floating to the surface like a black wounded jellyfish. I assumed that the combined effect of immersion in the water and the boat hook falling on his head unstuck the ghastly apparition. I watched long enough to ensure that the man could swim and then turned my attention to the main problem, which was that unless one of the boats moved the banging would continue unabated throughout the remainder of the night. The crew on the French boat were now much more concerned with retrieving their man overboard than they were with Shady Lady, so it was unlikely that a solution would come from the French boat.

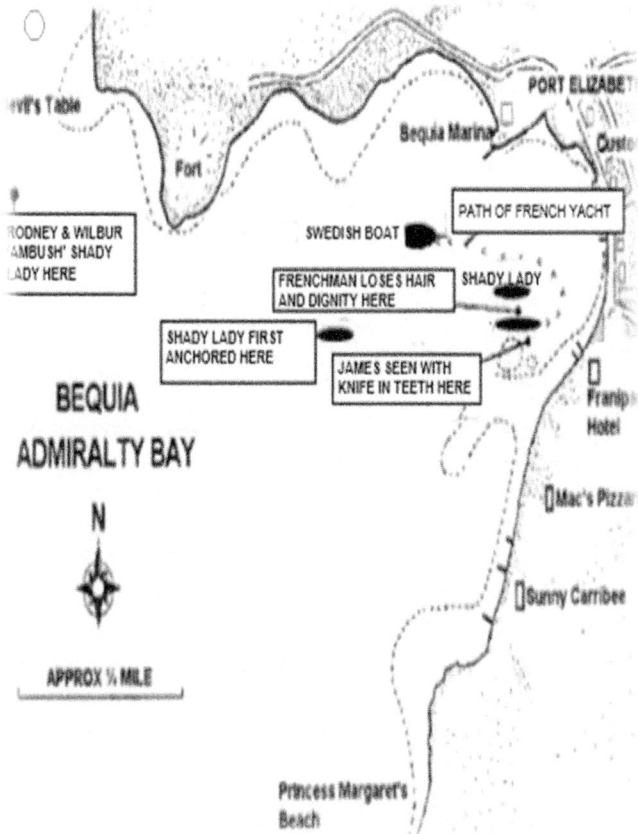

BEQUIA

ADMIRALTY BAY

N

APPROX ¼ MILE

"Well, I'm not going to move," I said.

Liz pursed her lips.

"James, there can only be one winner in a contest between fibreglass and concrete and that's not going to be us,"

"Anne put Fenders out," I remarked ignoring Liz's plea, "so they should take up any further impact,"   but I knew that Fenders wouldn't be enough.

I stroked my chin thoughtfully, "I know," I said.

"Let's bring the dinghy in from the stern and tie it to the side. If Frenchie boy there," I inclined my head in the direction of the French boat, which due to a wind change, was now several yards away and whose crew was just about to haul in a dripping, furious, and very bald Frenchman, "makes contact again, he'll scratch his freeboard on the rowlocks."

"Great idea," Liz agreed. "You're a genius."

"I know," I said. We made our way aft and we looked for the dinghy painter.

"Where's the dinghy?" I looked over the stern. There was nothing. I quickly walked around Shady Lady. There was no dinghy in sight.

I frowned, "Have you moved it?"

"Of course, I haven't moved it," growled Liz.

"Are you sure," and without waiting for an answer, "has Anne?"

"No, Anne hasn't touched it either," answered Liz.

"Did you tie it on properly?" she asked.

I thought back to the early evening. I knew I'd tied it securely, but I also knew that I hadn't locked it to Shady Lady with the steel painter provided for that purpose.

"Yes, of course, I tied it on properly," I answered irritably.

"Surely, they haven't pinched it," Liz peered into the gloom at the French boat.

"Well, if they have, they're in real trouble," I answered grimly.

"Not if they sail off before morning," answered Liz, almost to herself.

I thought about what she had said.

"I'm going in," I said.

"What?" Liz looked startled.

"I'm going to swim around the bastard's boat, to see if it's on the other side. If it's there, I'll bring it back."

Liz became alarmed. "Don't be silly. You couldn't reach their deck from the water, and if they had it, they'd certainly have it tied to the deck."

I noticed that the entire crew of the French boat seemed to have gone down below and, one by one, the cabin lights started to go out.

"I'll take a carving knife with me. I've a good mind to cut his bloody anchor rode too," I said in frustration.

Liz was even more alarmed.

68

"Don't be a bloody fool that could be dangerous, and besides, his anchor is attached to a chain, I heard it clatter down when they anchored," she said finally.

I realised she was right, but I also had to be sure that they didn't have the dinghy. I fetched the carving knife from the galley and silently slid down the aft ladder into the water. It was surprisingly warm. Carefully inserting the long knife into my mouth and making sure the sharp end pointed away from me, I swam towards the bow of the French boat, with the knife clamped firmly between my teeth.

I felt a bit foolish when I reached the other side and found only one dinghy in evidence, which belonged to the French boat.

I decided it would be quicker to swim right around the boat in order to get back to Shady Lady and it was while I was doing a silent doggy paddle, about ten yards from the starboard side of the concrete hull, that I heard a yelp from the French yacht. The little man, who was still completely bald, had obviously been calming himself down with a cigarette on the side away from Shady Lady and had spotted me swimming in the water. Within seconds the whole family was on deck again and pointing towards me. The young woman was saying something earnestly to the man. I caught the words "Allons, allons," and I saw her making stabbing signs.

It was then I realised that I must have looked rather threatening swimming around their boat, pirate fashion with a large knife between my teeth and plainly visible in the moonlight. I hurriedly changed to a crawl and gave the French yacht a very wide berth indeed, as I swam back to Shady Lady. Because of the detour, it took me some minutes to get back. I climbed the aft ladder, removing the knife as I did so Liz helped me on board.

"Well, you must have done something." she said in admiration, "because they're moving." I looked across at the French boat and heard the throb of the engine. I saw the young woman engage their electric windlass, which pulled up the anchor chain, and the vessel was underway. The Frenchman turned his boat in front of Shady Lady and passed about twenty feet away, headed in the direction of the sea.

As he drew level, the Frenchman put his finger to his head and shouted something quite impolite. Anne once more emerged from the depths of the cabin, looking extremely pugnacious. The Frenchman was concentrating so much on me, that he hadn't seen a large wooden hulled yacht that had swung around in the wind, clearly silhouetted by the lights on the shore, and was now completely blocking his path. I instinctively shouted a warning.

"Look out, you idiot," I pointed ahead of the Frenchman's yacht.

Plainly taking this as provocation, the little man left his wheel unattended and rushed to the side of his boat nearest to Shady Lady, where he performed a little jig, with his thumbs in his ears and tongue out.

"The man is bonkers," I said.

The young woman, who had been stowing away the anchor walked back towards the wheel. She suddenly realised why I'd shouted and turned around to look towards the bow. She turned back and yelled in desperation. "Andre, attention, attention," The Frenchman looked but he was far too late.

There was a sharp sound of splintering wood, and then a TWANG, as the Frenchman's fore-stay snapped under the impact, he'd ploughed into the bow of the wooden boat, removed the bowsprit in the action, and become tangled up with their anchor chain.

He clasped his bald head in his hands in disbelief.

"Mon Dieu," he cried plaintively, as two rather rough and belligerent-looking Swedish sailors appeared on the deck of the wooden boat.

Liz tugged at my arm.

"Time, we went to bed, I think," Anne had already gone down below again in disgust, and I felt that she was probably a little disappointed now that the battle was plainly at an end. Liz and I took one last look at the French boat; its mast was now leaning at an angle of forty-five degrees with the Swedes advancing ominously towards the instigator of the damage. I smiled, and then we howled with laughter. It took us some time to get to sleep, as one or the other of us kept having a fit of giggles. We'd both forgotten the missing dinghy.

I was somewhat chagrined to wake up at first light by a pounding on the hull.

Liz looked worried.

"It's the bloody Frenchman," I said as I swung aggressively out of bed, pulled on my still-wet shorts, and with gritted teeth, charged out of the cabin. I stopped short. In front of me was a fierce-looking bearded local, who was hanging onto the side of Shady Lady.

"This yer dinghy man?" He nodded his head in the direction of a small fibreglass boat, which was tied to his own inflatable. I looked and my heart jumped. It had Shady Lady 2 painted on the side.

"Yes," I answered, looking puzzled, "where did you find it?"

"Way out man, Way out," the black man pointed airily in the region of the western horizon. "You must've tied 'im bad," he explained.

I knew that I hadn't and that it was quite definitely secure when I left it, but I didn't feel that I'd achieve anything by arguing.

"Well, thank you very much," I said, trying to smile. It soon became obvious that the black man wasn't about to part-company without an exchange of cash, so I offered him a wet $10 dollar note from my pocket.

The man shook his head contemptuously.

"Noo man, I lost a whole day fishin' to get this boat for ye."

"How much," I asked grimly,

"$200," he growled. Eventually, the amount fell to $50, because I was able to convince him that we'd no more cash on board. The black man reluctantly parted with the dinghy after accepting the money with bad grace and sped off towards the shore.

I was glad to get the dinghy back at almost any price as without one we would have had to swim everywhere, and I shuddered at the thought of the cost of replacing the damn thing. When Wilbur and Rodney turned up to say good-bye, I told them what had happened.

"You shouldn't have given 'im anything," said Wilbur.

"He does it all the time, steals dinghies, then takes it back and demands $20 for findin' it," added Rodney.

I didn't wish to lose face by letting them know that I'd parted with $50, why doesn't someone report him to the police?" I asked.

Wilbur shrugged.

"They probably take a cut," he answered cynically. "In any case, the guy is a witness for the police in a murder, so they say they wanna keep 'im sweet."

"So, until he testifies," Liz, who had been listening from the cockpit, raised her eyebrows, "the police won't act against him?"

"Yea, another lesson learned in the rich tapestry of life," answered Anne, who had been listening in and grinning.

We sailed Shady Lady at about 10 a.m. The Swedes were working on the bow of their boat, and they gave a cheery wave. I suspected that they'd turned their disaster into a cash windfall.

THE ANTILLES

The Leeward Islands:

CHAPTER
8

"Those that sail the seas in the Caribbean,
Can relax and enjoy it, providing they don't sail."

*This is factual, having sailed all these islands. In the book
'Sailing with Silver' there are also some substantial details
of the islands, particularly those in the Windwards.*

The Leeward and Windward chains of islands are
collectively part of the Lessor Antilles and are arguably one
of the most beautiful areas of the world, with an average
temperature of 31 degrees Celsius all year round and with a
wind speed of 18 knots, mostly easterly. This makes it a
perfect area to sail as the islands run roughly north to south.

Originally the area was inhabited by the Arawak', an
Indian tribe that originated in South America. They were a
peaceable people who lived mainly on a diet of fish and had
few enemies. Subsequently, they were invaded by the Caribs',
also from South America, but this tribe was very different, in
that they stole the land from the Arawak' and exterminated
them so that by the time the Europeans arrived, there were
very few remaining The Caribs gave their name to the
Caribbean Sea and were very different from other indigenous
Indians in that they have blue eyes.

Once the Europeans arrived on the scene, firstly the
Spanish, then the French, British, Dutch, Swedes, and
Portuguese, the aggressive Caribs met much the same
treatment as they had handed out to the Arawak. There are a
few left in Jamaica and Dominica, but probably less than 100
in each place.

73

The Spanish and Portuguese did not stay, preferring the land mass of South America where they already had colonies, and could defend their land, also stolen from the indigenous tribes, such as the Inca.

The islands became economically very important, as it was found that the climate was particularly favourable for growing sugar cane. Because of this they became hotly contested by the Europeans, many of the islands changing hands several times, usually connected to the European wars. For instance, Saint Lucia in the Windward Islands changed hands between the British and the French fourteen times. Indeed, in the eighteenth century, so important was this island to the British economy that the government of Great Britain forced General Cornwallis to send half his army to Saint Lucia to prevent the French from invading it. This allowed General Washington to overcome his depleted force, which when blockaded by the French Navy, could no longer receive replacement rations or ammunition.

The islands in the **Leeward** chain are as follows: North to South

Anguilla is a self-administered British overseas territory. It is the most northerly of the Leeward Islands, lying east of Puerto Rico and the Virgin Islands and directly northwest of Saint Martin. One Christmas we anchored in a beautiful bay where we spent the whole holiday period. We never saw another human being, despite the bay being quite large. It was completely idyllic. Now Anguilla is the number one tourist spot for the northern Caribbean. The capital is called Valley.

Saba originally belonged to the Swedes and was subsequently ceded to the Dutch. It is a small mountainous island with two towns, you must travel to Top before you can go to Bottom. It has an airstrip cut out of the side of a cliff called Hells Gate and it's well-named There is a video on U-tube which puts you in the co-pilot seat when landing on the island, not to be seen by those worried about flying.

Saint Martin a French possession shares the island with the Dutch which is called **Sint Maarten**. Rather than going to war over the territory, the story goes that a Dutchman and a Frenchman set off walking the perimeter of

74

the island, one going west and the other east. When they met at the end of the walk a line was drawn from that point to the starting point, thus amicably separating the island into two parts. While the French have the larger part, the Dutch have the most important with the port of Philipsburg. It is a free port, so one can buy electrical goods, jewellery, and other expensive items free of tax. They also sport several large Casino's. The capital of the French side is called Marigot Bay, a quiet backwater with excellent restaurants.

Sint Eustatius is a Dutch island to the southwest of Sint Maarten and is quite different in that the people living on the island still wear Dutch clothes and clogs that were worn by the Dutch in the 1800's. Most are white and the architecture is very Dutch. It is almost as though the island hasn't moved past the nineteenth century. Sint Eustatius was the first country to recognise the new country of the United States of America. This is no surprise, as they benefited hugely during the American War of Independence, by allowing weapons to be shipped from their country to the American rebels. At that stage of their history, they were by far the richest island in the Caribbean bar, none.

Saint Barthelemy (St Barts) This island is only a 10-minute speed boat ride south from Sint Maarten and its main port and town is called Gustavia, which reminds one of Gulliver's Travels. It has a beautiful beach on the north side, where a restaurant and hotel are owned by the parents of the son who married Pippa Middleton, the sister of Kate Middleton.

Going south, **Rotunda** is a small uninhabited island that has a solitary British pillar box on it. If you post a letter there, you will have a unique postmark on your envelope when it arrives. What stamp one uses has never been explained, but apparently letters are collected from time to time.

Antigua and Barbuda are two islands southeast of St. Barts and Barbuda comes under the administration of Antigua. These were British islands until their independence in the early 1980's. Also, now members of the British Commonwealth. English harbour in the east is a favourite for sailors because it is virtually surrounded by land with quite a narrow entrance, so it is a good place to anchor if the sea is rough. Unfortunately, they have the worst customs in the Caribbean as one must stay in one's yacht until they decide to come to you. Sometimes this takes a whole day. It is now very much a tourist island with prices higher than most. Nelson used to anchor in English Harbour, the gossip is that he had a mistress there. 'Harbour' is a bit of a misnomer as there is no actual harbour structure in the bay.

Barbuda administered by Antigua in the south can be reached only from Antigua, as one must clear customs there first. The whole of Barbuda was originally a sugar estate owned by the Boddington who have a large estate just north of Bath. When we lived in Bath, I used to fly over their huge mansion before landing at the racecourse nearby where I sometimes kept my aircraft. It always brought back to me how they made their money, as Barbuda was the only area in the world that bred African slaves for the slave market. When we were sailing in the Caribbean, the island had been taken over by the mafia, no doubt as a staging post for drugs. A friend of ours who sailed there was met with several bullets which pierced his sails. He made a speedy retreat.

St Kitts and Nevis are a popular hideaway for the Royal family, particularly Prince Charles. Probably the strongest British fortress in the Leeward or Windward islands is now a ruin but still a substantial military property. Originally occupied by the French and British, after much fighting the islands were ceded to the British in 1713 and it became the most profitable in the whole of the Antilles. It gained independence in 1983 and is part of the Commonwealth. In 1998 Hurricane Georges caused 458 million pounds worth of damage there.

Guadeloupe is a French Island southeast of Antigua and is a Department of France along with small islands to the south of it, including Marie Galante and Ill des Saintes. This is where Christopher Columbus first found the Pineapple. It has one of the largest population's in the Leeward chain and the currency is the Euro.

Il Des Saintes are islands just south of Guadeloupe and administered by them. It is a delight to visit overnight as a sailor, as after checking in to the police station the next morning, one can buy hot chocolate croissants from the bakery next door. These islands have a notable history in that this is where the British and French fleet met in the Battle of the Saintes in 1782. The British thrashed the French capturing four of their main galleons including the flagship containing the French commander. This put an end to a joint French and Spanish threat to invade Jamaica. The importance of this battle, however, was that Admiral Rodney was credited with the tactic of 'breaking the line.' Subsequently, this was used by Nelson in the Battle of Trafalgar and even later by Admiral Jellico in the battle of Jutland. Rodney did not deserve the credit, as he was in fact in his cabin below with gout. It was due to his second in command, who was friendly with a man called Sir John Clerk who lived in Edinburgh. Clerk had never been to sea, but despite this, he was very interested in naval tactics and over several dinners with various naval officers he proved his theory by war gaming on his small pool in his garden.

Montserrat island is southwest of Guadeloupe and is still British. It was well known for hosting various music groups in the 60's and 70's as they had first-class facilities with a modern sound studio. This attracted the Beatles, Rolling Stones, and many others. Recently it suffered a cataclysmic volcanic eruption that destroyed part of the island, and the British Navy was called in to remove inhabitants from the area.

Dominica not to be confused with the Dominican Republic, is the southernmost island in the Leeward chain and was given their independence by Britain in 1976. It is a member of the commonwealth and possibly the most primitive of the islands having a large rain forest in the interior. It was ceded to Britain from the French after the seven year war in 1713. It does not have good holding for yachts outside the capital of Roseau. Elizabeth and I anchored there once after a day's sail. The next morning, we found that we had drifted about a mile out to sea. Fortunately, there were no rocks in the area, or I wouldn't be telling you this story today.

THE WINDWARD ISLANDS

CHAPTER
9

"As long as you miss the reefs, the rocks, other boats,
Hurricanes, storms, thieves, and boat boys, you'll have a
great time."

*This too is factual having sailed around all these
islands.*

Martinique. Although held by the British at various
times in history, Martinique is now definitely French. This is
the island where Josephine, Emperor Napoleon's, wife was
born. It is a Department of France, which means that they
vote in the Presidential elections carried out on the mainland
of France. It is by far the most sophisticated island in the
Antilles. The island was traded by the British in 1815 and it
has remained French since then.

Mont Pelée, the volcano in the north of the island
erupted in 1902 and destroyed St. Pierre, a north eastern
coastal town, killing over 30,000 people. The mayor of the
town refused the inhabitants to flee Saint-Pierre, and all
died except Auguste Cyparis, a prisoner in a thickly walled
cell below ground, he was the only person the survive.

Diamond Rock is about an hour's sail due west from
St. Anne. Shaped like the top of a bullet, it lifts sheer out of
the sea to a height of about 500 feet. The distance between
the south end of Martinique and the rock is only a few
hundred yards, but the water between is deep enough to sail
through safely.

While Silver Star was passing the rock to the port side,

78

before turning south towards St. Lucia, I told the guests that some hundreds of British troops had captured the rock during the Napoleonic wars, and it had been a severe embarrassment to the French. The main reason for the capture was because some British military wag had decided that as there were no mosquitoes on the rock, it would be an ideal site for a hospital for sick troops based in St. Lucia. It was correct that there were no mosquitoes there, but the place was and still is apparently, infested with the deadly fer-de-lance snake. More British troops died from snake bites than they would have done from yellow fever.

Viewed from the sea it was difficult to imagine how they landed, never mind lived on the place, and impossible to imagine them pulling a heavy cannon up to the top, but they did. It was the only rock in the world at that time commissioned as a ship and it became HMS Diamond Rock. This annoyed Napoleon no end as his darling Josephine came from Martinique. To redress French honour Napoleon sent the French fleet under Admiral Villeneuve to remove the Brits.

Despite Nelson chasing him all the way there, he completed the job, and the occupation of Diamond Rock came to an inglorious end after only eighteen months of annexation.

Because Villeneuve had wisely chosen not to fight Nelson, Napoleon ordered him to return to France in disgrace. This stinging rebuke encouraged him to put to sea again rather earlier than he had contemplated and before the fleet was ready, the result was the Battle of Trafalgar.

The funnier story, which I enjoyed telling about the rock, came much later, however. In 1978, just before St Lucia became an independent country, some Brits and South Africans had been celebrating the New Year. The story of Diamond Rock had come up and for a dare, a dozen or so men set out from St. Lucia before first light in a fast motor boat. Their equipment included climbing gear and a huge Union Jack. By 10 in the morning, the British flag flew from the top of Diamond Rock for all to see.

Had that been all there was to it; a rather headstrong prank, it would have passed by without becoming an

79

International incident. What the Brits and South Africans didn't know was that the senior admiral of the French navy had chosen that day to visit Fort de France, the capital of Martinique, and was sailing in from the Atlantic just as the British flag was raised.

There are stories that the poor man almost had an apoplectic fit and he immediately ordered the marines to go in and remove the invaders. Unfortunately, the French marines had no climbing gear, so could only glower from the sea at the jeering throng on top, who were making unkind suggestions about the efficiency of the French Navy.

Now, of course, the whole thing had got out of hand, with a French cruiser and destroyer standing by at vast cost while twelve cold, hungry, and now worried Brits and South Africans stood their ground afraid to go down amongst the tough marines at whom they'd been hurling insults. In the end, the French sent in armed police paratroopers in helicopters. The offenders were slung in jail and subsequently deported. The French had the last laugh, because by the time the deported pranksters had bought their tickets to travel back to St. Lucia, the island had become independent, and they were denied entry into the new country.

SAINT LUCIA. The next island south is Saint Lucia, an island that changed hands fourteen times between the British and the French. It became so important that General Cornwallis in America, was ordered to send almost half his troops to Saint Lucia to defend it against the French. No doubt it created a situation that gave the American rebels under Washington a great opportunity, which they used to good effect.

The capital Castries is still named after Admiral Castries, a French Governor. It is a pretty island and is now well-known as a tourist spot. Most of the major hotels are in the northwest of the island although the international airport is in the south. It has an open volcano near the town of Soufrière in the southwest and the well-known two Pitons which feature on the national flag, are just south of the town and over shadow it. The centre of the island is mountainous, as are most of the larger Caribbean islands, except for Barbados which is well to the east of the Windward Islands and is not generally included in the chain.

SAINT VINCENT & THE GRENADINES

St Vincent is about 38 sea miles from the bottom of St Lucia. It is best known for hosting many international banks which some have accused of dodgy practices. Like most of the Caribbean Islands, the country has been owned by the French and the English, finally ceded to Britain in 1783. Before then it was a haven for escaping slaves from Barbados and St Lucia. These mixed with the original owners, the Caribs, and created some problems for the British who eventually expelled them to a tiny island called Baliceaux just off the coast of Bequia. Subsequently, they were moved to an island off the South American coast. At the time of writing, Baliceaux is for sale for thirty million dollars and is currently uninhabited. Saint Vincent has a large volcano in the north of the island that last erupted in 1979, causing huge damage to the area. There are a couple of stories about what happened on the island in my book 'Sailing on Silver'.

The first major island south is **Bequia**, an absolute delight, particularly for sailors. Bequia has one of the largest natural harbours in the Antilles and because the bay is in the shape of a horseshoe facing west, it is an ideal anchorage. The people of Bequia are reputed to be the only people worldwide to be authorised by Greenpeace to catch whales. They usually only kill one a year and land it on a small island south of Bequia called Petit Nevis. There is much more of this story in 'Sailing on Silver'.

The Grenadines are several islands south of Saint Vincent and administered by them. The first major island is **Mustique,** very well-known for its inhabitants. Princess Margaret had a house there, as did the Rolling Stones and various other celebrities. The island was bought by Lord Glenconner, better known as Colin Tennant. Colin bought the island from a Saint Vincent lawyer for £25,000 and turned it into one of the most exclusive places to live on the planet. I knew him well as I also knew the daughter of the lawyer who sold him the island. It has a small hotel there called the Cotton House and the place to eat is Basil's Bar in the bay on the west side of the island. There is an excellent book on Glenconnor's life, written by Nicholas Courtney and it is worth reading. I also knew the ex-chairman of the Mustique company which was owned by Colin Tennant, and it was run by one of the sons of Field Marshall Alexander. The last time I sailed there was in the company of the man who put together the famous Indian temple in the garden of Colin Tennant's house. It is still there. If you are sailing in the Grenadines, Mustique is well worth a visit, but if you are anchoring opposite Basil's Bar, put out a rear anchor as it rolls during the night, often giving the impression that you have enjoyed yourself too much at Basil's Bar. There are a few stories about Mustique in Sailing on Silver.

There are some small uninhabited islands south of Mustique, but the next main one down is called **Canouan** which is only about 3.5 miles long by 1.25 miles wide. It was sparsely inhabited when we were sailing there, but I understand that some progress has been made to make it attractive to tourists. It has a beautiful long bay with a sandy beach but was not good for yachts to moor.

Just south of Canouan is the island of **Mayreau** which has a small, sheltered bay on its north end. It will only fit a few yachts in there, but it's great for swimming. There is also a small open-air restaurant that is open in the season.

The east of Mayreau are four small, inhabited islands that lead to **Tobago Cays**. This was a must to visit as it had a superb coral reef and very good holding for yachts. Unfortunately, the last time we were there, the coral had died.

Union Island about 8 miles southwest of Tobago Cays is where one can re-provision. The island is very French, although now under the auspices of St. Vincent.

They have a small airport there which brings in day trippers. The airport is tucked under a hill, so aircraft must dive quite steeply to land, and if it goes too fast, you're in the sea.

Palm Island is situated to the east of Union and sports a small hotel and a few houses. It has arguably the nicest beach in the Antilles, it being pink in colour. One can moor there, but usually not for an overnight stay.

Petit St Vincent is the last island in the Grenadine chain, belonging to St. Vincent. This island is completely taken over by a hotel. If you can afford to stay there, you are allocated a chalet and can order what you need by raising a flag outside your door. The restaurant is excellent. The last time we were there with our grandchildren we sat next to Daniel Craig with a partner, much to their excitement. The bay is enclosed by a reef at the eastern end with the island of Petit Martinique opposite, which is governed by the large Island of Grenada. The holding for yachts is very good and arguably one of the nicest anchorages in the Antilles.

Petit Martinique Despite the name, Petit Martinique is administered by Grenada. There used to be substantial smuggling between the islands north, but the Communist government, defeated by the US forces, ensured it was more settled. Sailing south one should book with the customs on the island, called **Carriacou** where they have a customs post. There is also a hurricane hole there which one should head for if a hurricane is included in the weather forecast. There is also a pleasant bay there, called Tyrell Bay but most head straight for Grenada. Kick 'em Jenny is just off the coast to the west, where there is an undersea volcano. The story is, should it erupt, it could wipe out most of the Antilles. I was informed that it is a similar size to the underground volcano at Yellowstone Park in the USA.

Grenada. This island, named 'the spice island' is roughly the same size as St. Lucia or St. Vincent. We used to sail to the south of the island to a bay called Prickly Bay. It is many years since we sailed there, but we were warned not to anchor in Saint Georges, the capital. Since the US invasion, I am sure there have been many changes. The people are very welcoming and there are some first-class restaurants on the island.

They have a large airport there, which was built by the Cubans, and was the source of all the troubles.

THE U-BOAT AFFAIR

The Retribution from the Royal Navy

CHAPTER
10

"Before you judge a man, walk a mile in his shoes.
After that who cares?... He's a mile away and you've got his
shoes!"

Billy Connolly

---

*This story is from a chapter from Sailing on Silver,
Part II, which includes a visit from Michael Caine and
Billy Connolly and their partners.*

Despite the start-up difficulties, the restaurant was
now doing well, and we began to get a good reputation for
excellent food. Providing we could keep Yani sober, and well
away from the female staff, we reckoned we could not go
wrong a rather naive conclusion.

At this time, two famous actors were filming a comedy
in the south end of the island, and we got a call one day to
ask us if they could come to lunch with their wives. We didn't
usually make lunches at that time, but given their celebrity
status, we agreed to put on a special meal. Once one opens a
restaurant, you cannot close it to others, and as there was a
Royal Naval Destroyer on a goodwill visit to Castries at that
time, we had some sailors who dropped in for a drink.

They spotted the celebrities, and we were concerned

85

that Royal Naval autograph hunters would ruin their meal, but they took it all in good part.

The sailors were delighted and promised that they would return with their mates the same evening. They explained that it was to be their last evening on St Lucia, as their ship was moving off south the next day.

From time to time, yachtsmen who were travelling back home, would leave their yachts in the lagoon near to the Yachtsman's Bar, and ask us to keep an eye on them while they were gone. I was always careful to warn them that we could not be responsible for these boats. If someone paid a fee for their boat tied to our dock, then that was different.

Someone who I had met while sailing owned a small Catamaran. One evening about two weeks before the celebrities' lunch, he had come and told me he and his girlfriend were going to the States for a couple of weeks and would I keep an eye on the boat which he had moored about fifty yards off our dock. I had nodded my assent with the usual warning. It was quite easy to see from the bar, and it was the only Catamaran in the lagoon at the time.

The night after the lunch, the sailors duly arrived with about ten others and were soon in good spirits. The bar area started to fill up when I noticed a man called Kruger chug up to our dock in a dinghy. Kruger was an infrequent visitor because he used to charter quite a lot down in the Grenadines. I assumed when I saw him that he must have dropped off some charter guests in St Lucia. He always had his dog with him that looked as old, ragged, and dirty as Kruger did.

I did not particularly like him, as not only was he a scruffy individual, but after a few drinks he would use foul language, which of course did not go down well with female guests within earshot. Kruger owned quite a large Catamaran called Rosie, which took about six guests, but I never came across anyone who sailed with him, so did not know whether he ran a good boat or not. If his personal cleanliness was anything to go by, I doubted it.

Kruger was normally a surly individual and drank on his own, but as soon as he saw the sailors, he made a beeline for their party. At first, they ignored him, but I noticed as the evening wore on, they had included him in the general chat and merriment that was going on. It was near 1 a.m. when I sensed the conversation was turning a little unfriendly, and I moved nearer so that I could overhear what was said.

Kruger sneered and waved his hand away from his body. 'Ze British navy is useless, I know, I fought zem in ze war.'

"Oh yes matey,' said one sailor 'and what did you do?' Kruger put his right hand on his chest 'I vas ze man who sank ze Royal Oak battleship,"

"You sank a battleship?" said another incredulously.

"Me, I sank the Royal Oak, wiz all the crew on board," he banged down his beer glass on the bar counter.

It was clear, they didn't believe Kruger. "Oh yeah, what did you use mate, a shotgun?" There were general guffaws.

Kruger shook his head, staggered slightly poking a rating in the stomach.

"Pow, pow' he said, 'I vas ze torpedo officer on U-boat U47 und've got into Scapa Flow, und ve sank the bastards, it vas on 14th October 1939." He grinned.

Suddenly one of the sailors realised that what Kruger was saying was correct.

"My uncle was on that ship mate, you killed him, you fucking...'

I quickly intervened, by buying the sailors a free round, and with a friend, we got hold of the drunken Kruger and steered him back to his dinghy. He apparently did not wish to go, but I told him that he was not welcome to stay while the sailors were there, and I strongly advised him to get back to his boat while still in one piece. As we helped him into the dinghy, his dog bit me for my pains. I got hold of it and threw it in after him. When he had gone, I really thought that was the last of it. I remember one of the sailors asking me what Kruger sailed, and I told them he sailed in a catamaran.

"Ah, thought the bugger couldn't sail a proper boat," was all he said.

The next morning, I was checking something in the bar, when I looked out into the lagoon. Something was wrong, I thought, but could not quite place what it was. I suddenly realised with a start that something was different. The catamaran belonging to my American friend had gone. I frowned as I walked over nearer to the window.

"Oh Jesus," I said.

"What's the problem?" Liz asked as she walked through to the bar.

"Isn't that a mast sticking out of the water?" I asked as I pointed my finger at where the catamaran had been.

"Good Lord, it's sunk," answered Liz.

"Or it has been sunk,"

"What do you mean?" Liz looked at me in surprise.

I told her about the near-fracas the night before and what Kruger had said. "I'll bet you anything that they sank the catamaran after they left the Restaurant last night..."

"But that's not Kruger's boat," said Liz, "that's..."

"I know, the stupid buggers have sunk the wrong one." Our American friend returned to the island within a couple of days, and I pointed out that I had simply found the vessel had sunk one morning, I decided not to tell him of my suspicions.

Once refloated, he said he found the water had come in through two faulty seacocks, which he was sure he had checked before he left for the States. He never did learn what might have happened, and what I believe did happen. Members of Her Majesty's Navy had almost certainly sunk the catamaran. I hoped it was good practice for them because they were shortly to go to the Falklands.

THE YACHT RACE

CHAPTER

11

"The chance for mistakes is about equal to the number of
crew squared."
Ted Turner

Another chapter from sailing on Silver - Part II

Shortly after the catamaran incident, I was talking to
an old yachting friend of mine, Jasper Cartwright, who was
an engineer for a new yacht chartering company in Rodney
Bay Lagoon. We were lamenting that there was no yacht
racing on the island.

We had organised one or two small affairs when
chartering, but the races were between the two charter
companies concerned and included only three or four boats.

"Why don't we organise a major yacht race ourselves
for all comers?" I asked, we talked some more about the idea
and Jasper became quite enthusiastic. We felt we should run
races under the auspices of the local yacht club of which we
were both members, so we decided to seek out the opinion of
the then secretary.

Tracking him down, we carefully outlined the idea of
a three-day yacht race to Martinique. St Lucia had a public
holiday coming up, which always fell on a Thursday, so we
reasoned it would not be too difficult for most interested
people to get the Friday off, making a long weekend of it.

The secretary listened to us in silence. Then he frowned as he spoke.

"But, if you have yacht racing man, it will interfere with the social side of the yacht club."

I looked at him in surprise. "But you're a yacht club, which means that you should be promoting the sailing of yachts."

"Noo man, we don't want any smelly yachtsmen around here, this club is a nice club, we can bring our wives and children for lunch at the weekend and lie on the beach, what do we want to organise yacht racing for?"

Well, he had a point. It was obvious the St Lucia Yacht Club, whatever its beginnings had become a social club and it seemed as though the members did not want to change it.

On the way back to the Pub with Jasper, I started to formulate an idea.

"Why don't we start our own club?" I suggested.

"What, you mean a yacht club in competition with the yacht club?" He grinned at the thought.

"Not really," I answered, "our club would be solely for yachtsmen and should encourage offshore yacht racing."

"But we couldn't possibly afford a club house..." Jasper looked thoughtful as he said it.

"No need, we could use the yachtsmen's Haven bar at the Pub, I'm sure Liz would agree to it, the room is quite large, it is not being used, and the drinks licence is already set up..."

We went to the Pub and had a look at the room I had suggested, and as Liz seemed quite keen, we agreed to go ahead with the project. The St Lucia Yachting Association was born. Jasper became the first secretary, me the treasurer, and we invited a prominent St Lucian to become Commodore. Within a few weeks we had over sixty members. We both realised however, that it was important to get the first race off the ground and so I suggested to Liz that the Pub sponsor the three-day race to Martinique, which I had originally suggested to the St Lucia Yacht Club.

There seemed to be a substantial amount of enthusiasm for this proposed race, as there was something in it for everyone. Yacht racing for the keenest, Club Med and

90

the Martinican girls for those keen in another directions, and shopping in Martinique for the rest, the latter was probably the biggest draw of all.

It was agreed that the starting area would be between two temporary buoys which we would lay in Rodney Bay, and that a motor launch would proceed us to St Anne's on the south-eastern part of Martinique and drop the two same starting buoys to act as a finishing line. St Anne's would be the anchorage for the first night, and I telephoned Club Med and asked them if they would allow the participants in the race to utilise the hotel facilities. Their answer was in the affirmative, so the first leg of the race was set.

We decided that the second leg on the Friday would be a downwind leg from St Anne's to Diamond Rock on the south western end of Martinique, then north into Fort de France Bay, finishing between the same buoys planted by the motor launch which would set off from St Anne's early on the Friday morning. To make the start in St Anne's more fun. I invented what I think was the first 'Le Mans' start for Yachts.

The idea being that all racing yachts would be moored just off St Anne's beach, and on a gun being fired, the skipper and one other would jump into the water, swim for the shore, retrieve a coloured ribbon tied to a palm tree, and swim back to the boat. No one on the yachts would be allowed to make any preparations for sailing until the two swimmers were firmly back on board. Then the anchor had to be pulled up and sail raised, no engines were allowed of course. This method of starting was to cause much hilarity and confusion as we shall see.

Once the second leg had been completed, the yachts were to be free to moor either in Anse Mitan (on the south side of Fort de France Bay) or Fort de France itself, Fort de France being the capital city of Martinique situated on the north side of the Bay.

The Saturday was to be completely free for shopping, and Sunday would be the third and last leg of the race, with a start in Fort de France Bay and the finish in Rodney Bay.

We decided that each leg would have a winner, and then there would be an overall winner for the three races. The Pub would give the major prize, and we trawled around various companies in Castries until we had all the other sponsors. I was keen to get the Martinique Yacht Club involved, so waiting for a day when I knew Freddy the Fart was not flying; I hitched a lift on one of the St Lucia Airways charter flights and had a meeting with the Commodore and secretary of the Yacht club there. The Martinicans were delighted that St Lucia was going to organise races again, and soon there was to be a good liaison between the two organisations. The upshot of my visit was that the French insisted on hosting a party for us on a Saturday night, with food and music laid on.

As preparations continued, we realised we had another problem. The boats that were being entered for the race were a polyglot of charter boats and private entries, ranging from a sixty-footer to a thirty-four-footer. For those of you who are uninitiated in the ways of sailing boats the physics of speed of boats under sail are in direct proportion to the waterline length. This meant that to give the smaller boats at least half a chance of winning, we needed to invent some sort of handicap system. I worked out a small programme on my computer, and we fed all sorts of magical figures into it. If the result did not seem fair, we added a fudge factor to adjust. It was all very unscientific, but in practice worked quite well.

By the time the day came, we were delighted to have fifteen entries. Some charter companies had entered their own boat, but had also been generous enough to charter out their yachts at a reasonable price to locals wanting to join in. I had been offered a Sparkman and Stevens forty-four from Sunshine which was quite a fast cruiser. I had picked a team that consisted of a young American boy I knew called Brodie, two St. Lucians from the Sunshine dock crew, Archibald, Liz's business partner, Brodie's St. Lucian girlfriend, Philippa, and another girl called Angie who was half British and half Arab.

Jasper, who was the favourite to win had a forty-three-foot yacht, built in Argentina called Eleanor, it was sleek and fast, and he was my main target.

There was one small yacht sailing which caused much mirth because all the men on board were considered 'light on their feet' They were all Europeans, and as I knew them all quite well, I didn't believe a word of the malicious rumour.

Nevertheless, their yacht was christened Aphrodite by the rest. Certainly, they were the least experienced bunch of sailors in the race.

Rodney Bay seems quite large until there are fifteen large yachts in it jockeying for position. The start line was about ten yachts wide, and the idea was to have a running start downwind. This meant that we had to position the yacht in the water so that we would cross the line about two or three seconds after the gun. If a yacht went through early, then it had to return and go through again. If it was left too late of course, then all that would be seen would be the sterns of all the other yachts sailing off into the distance, the gun went off as I was some hundred yards from the line. It had been interesting watching; how different skippers approached the problem of starting. One of the yachts Keep Me, kept going through the line beforehand and swiftly gybing thus going around in a perpetual circle. To turn a yacht in a complete circle means that the jib lines must be transferred from one side of the boat to the other, twice for each circle, and each time the newly positioned foresail must be winched in. The main is easier because the boom, on which the main sits, is simply allowed to move across with the wind. Nevertheless, it is prudent to reel in the slack on the main sheet (main sail) otherwise the boom travels with too much force, and there is a danger of it ripping off the mast.

Unfortunately, for the crew of Keep Me Young, the skipper decided to try these gyrations about ten minutes before the start. Perhaps his watch was fast. The first circle was carried out in an exemplary manner, but we noticed a fast deterioration in the crew handling by the third circle. The yacht went through the line for the fourth time just ahead of the gun, and in their effort to turn quickly, when the yacht came about, the person allocated the job of looking after the main, had clearly run out of steam, or had lost concentration (or both). As he realised the boat was gybing, and the line running through his hands because of the wind force on the sail, he must have attempted to hold on to the line, with painful results. We heard a yelp from the yacht, and as the boom came swinging around at some considerable speed, it completely wrenched off the mast. Unfortunately, by this time, the culprit yacht was blocking part of the start line, so others had to swerve to avoid the stricken vessel. One yacht called Lady Penelope, ploughed into the stern of it, the force knocking the skipper of Keep Me Young, who was by then beside himself with anguish, straight into the water.

We had kept well clear, but I was disappointed that Jasper crossed the line just in front of us. We were so close that one could almost touch the stern of Jasper's yacht from the bow of our own. Jasper was so pleased to have beaten us, that he turned and gave me a 'V' sign. As did he so he took his attention away from his direction for a split second. The wind changed slightly, and I saw his boom lazily arching across in a gybe. On the deck was a young man, a relative of Jasper's who had gone along for the ride. He was standing on the starboard side of the deck looking towards the tangle of yachts behind. He never saw the boom, and no doubt did not know what force propelled him into the water, where he landed quite unhurt. Of course, it was a rule that a man overboard had to be picked up, which not only meant Jasper had to turn his boat around to do that, but because of the considerable gaggle of yachts now coming up to the starting line, he would have to wait for them all to go through before he could get the unfortunate youth back on board. Jasper was not a happy man as we sailed past him waving frantically and cheering at the top of our voices.

Despite the difficulties caused by Keep Me Young the yacht with the separated boom, it was surprising how quickly the field got sorted out. We led the race past Pigeon Island on the westernmost part of Rodney Bay and turned to starboard. The wind in the Eastern Caribbean is predominantly from the east, and as we were to turn northeast when clearing the northern end of St Lucia, it was going to be a hard beat up to St Anne's, and we knew we may have to tack several times to get to the finishing line. The wind speed was about twenty-five knots, and the seas ran around seven feet, which was about normal.

The sail took just over five hours, and we were passed

by two faster boats, but on handicap we came second, which pleased us no end, as none of our crew had raced together before.

The last boat in was the one dubbed 'Aphrodite' which arrived some two hours later. Because of the size of their yacht, they had taken quite a drubbing in the channel, and I was told that the sea had washed down below more than once, making their bunks sopping wet. There was much hilarity over this of course, with comments like, 'that will curb the buggers.'

Club Med gave us a great welcome, and for those that have not read my book A Shitty Day in Paradise, I should explain that Club Med does not normally allow anyone but hotel guests to participate in their activities. This is because the residents are given beads with which to purchase drinks, money not being acceptable in the bars. Also, meals are paid for in the price of the deal. In our case we arranged beforehand for dinners to be laid on for everyone, and we paid in advance. Yachtsmen could buy beads at the reception desk, and so a good time was had by all. Club Med have a show in the evening which is put on by the staff and sometimes guests are inveigled to join in. It is usually excellent, and we thoroughly enjoyed it. On the way back to the boat, we noticed several 'notables' from St Lucia taking a dinghy back to their boat, packed with unfamiliar young females. Their wives had been left at home.

l also saw a couple of people off the yacht called Lady Penelope snorkelling, which I thought rather odd in the dark, but did not think any more about it until after the start the next morning.

Yacht racing is extremely hard work. The adrenaline that one feels coupled with the fresh air, the sea and the physical exertion ensures a good night's sleep. This together with the wine and good food, guaranteed that I slept like a log that night, and thus was not aware of all sorts of sexual shenanigans going on in the cabins next to mine.

I woke early and went on deck. The sun had just risen, and it was obviously going to be a beautiful day, there being not a cloud in the sky. I looked either side of me and was surprised to see that the yacht which had the separated boom, Keep Me Young, was moored about three boats up from ours. They must have had the offending part repaired and sailed up after dark.

All the boats were moored bow to the beach, and I noticed two were very close to the land no doubt in the hope that the shorter the swim for the two crew, the faster the take-off. As I went below, I saw Brodie's girlfriend coming out of a cabin that was certainly not Brodie's, and shortly afterwards I was to see Angie appearing out of another cabin which was inhabited by the two St Lucian's. She looked quite pleased with herself. Quite what had gone on, I was never to find out, but the St Lucian males were quite useless that day, they seemed to be completely drained... In future races, I was to make myself unpopular by segregating the males from the females.

The gun was fired, and there were splashes as we all dived for the water. I have always been a strong swimmer, but I realised that the two yachts that moored closer to the beach would be first away. The other swimmer from my boat was Angie, who beat me to the shore, got her ribbon and raced past me heading for the water. Clearly whatever had gone on the night before had not sapped her energy...

I had a bit of difficult untying my ribbon, and I could hear the crescendo of my crew urging me on. At last, I loosened it and sprinted back down the beach. Within a couple of minutes, I was hauled on board, breathless, with the ribbon firmly clenched in my teeth. Such was the excitement that it was over ten minutes later, before I realised that it was still there.

The Aphrodite boat was the nearest to the shore, and as they drew in their anchor, while at the same time putting up their sails, I could see them headed for disaster. Sure enough, they had not left themselves enough space to turn and they went hurtling straight for the beach and were lodged solidly into the sand when I last saw them. They were followed soon after by the other yacht that had moored close in, and there was much merriment on the other boats as these rather comical scenes unfolded in front of our eyes. There is nothing quite so funny as a beached yacht with part of the crew in the water frantically trying to push the hull back into deeper water while the rest of the crew on deck attempted to give unhelpful advice.

We had stayed a reasonable distance from the shore, and while this meant a longer swim, we were easily able to turn to starboard as soon as our anchor was up.

We were slightly behind the boat next to us on the port side, but as they had pulled their anchor rode too quickly, and the forward motion had taken them too far into the beach it allowed us to get away before them, although they managed to free themselves quickly afterward.

There were two more boats further to port, one of them turned to port and the other to starboard, with all the attendant crunches, sounds of metal upon metal, and human voices cursing that is normal in collisions at sea. When the confusion sorted itself out, we found we were a third away Keep Me Young was just in front of us.

The crew, of Keep Me Young had done well to get away so quickly but even though they were under full sail, they suddenly came to a shuddering stop. It was quite funny and so unexpected the people on board fell over with the force of the halt. I narrowly missed ploughing into their stern and was as puzzled as they obviously were that they had stopped. I knew there was no reef in that spot so certainly they could not have hit anything.

That evening when we all got together, I learned what the snorkellers the previous night had been up to. They had obviously tied a line around the propeller of Keep Me Young and fastened it to some underwater mooring which had been originally placed there by Club Med for a heavy vessel to be secured to. The crew of Lady Penelope who had got tangled up with Keep Me Young at the start in St Lucia no doubt thought some retribution was due.

Lady Penelope sailed past Keep Me Young, and the whole crew cheered and laughed, throwing balloons filled with water and flour. Before the end of the race, they were to wish they had not been so obvious in their exuberance.

We were now second to Jasper, who had turned to starboard out of the bay and was down winding parallel with the south end of Martinique. He had a large blooper (A very large foresail, that does a similar job to a spinnaker, but is much larger and heavier) and was really moving away from us quite quickly. We turned the corner to follow him, but because we had no blooper or spinnakers, we put up another main and poled it out on the other side in a method called wing on wing. We still had a large jib, and I was satisfied that once we had set our sails, we would keep up with the boat in front of us, blooper, or no blooper.

The other yachts were strung out behind us, and I was feeling pleased with our progress when disaster struck. The pole that held out the second mainsail buckled when there was a slight change of wind, and the port main came crashing onto the deck and ripped down the middle. We quickly took the whole gear down and straightened the pole out, putting it between two dinghy oars and lashing them to act like a splint on a broken arm. I shouted for the torn main sail to be shoved below, and for our other spare to be brought up. Fortunately, we had anticipated problems and we had a third main sail on board, stowed below in the forward sail locker.

I yelled to Angie who was the only one not gainfully employed at the time.

"Get the sheet, get the sheet, quickly," I could see that we were being overhauled by yachts that had started after us.

Angie rushed down below and came back up carrying what we discovered were bed sheets.

"Not the bloody bed sheets," I yelled unkindly, "we can't sail with them, can we?"

By this time, Angie had unfolded one of the sheets, and the wind had caught it taking it overboard. "That's bloody down to you," I shouted unkindly.

I should say here that yacht racing either brings the best out in one... or the worst, with me it was quite definitely the latter.

"We'll have to go back for it," shouted Angie, no doubt worried about the cost of replacing the article now floating gracefully on the sea like some huge Manta Ray.

"Not likely," I growled, as I noticed another yacht coming abeam of us, their crew annoyingly amused at our antics.

Brodie had taken the ripped main below and was just coming back with the new one, when Angie simply jumped off the stern.

I was furious and wished I had not suggested she would have to pay for the bed sheet now floating some five-hundred-yard s away.

We had no choice, of course, we had to gybe, and go and pick her up with the bed sheet she'd retrieved. While this was going on, we had the humiliation of Aphrodite sailing past us, who had at last got free of the beach. Their crew waved and jeered. "Don't worry about losing your bedding, you can sleep with us tonight," one shouted, "Running out of sails?" Shouted another.

I scowled and gave them a rude sign as we passed going in the wrong direction.

It took us a further two hours to reach Diamond Rock on the southwest corner of Martinique, and because of the delay, we were now trailing seventh. I gained a bit of time going between Diamond Rock and the mainland, some of the others, not knowing the area, left the Rock to starboard. Once we had passed the Rock, we turned north for the short sail up to Fort de France Bay, and on reaching it; we headed for the finishing line some four miles east into the bay. Because we were now into the wind, we had a substantial amount of tacking to do, and we eventually crossed the line sixth, having made up one place.

The night was a 'free' one, when everyone went their own way, to do their own thing. We had anchored in Fort de France so that we could transfer our substantial shopping more easily the next morning, and we were just about to leave the boat to head out to a local restaurant when we were hailed by two men in a large tender.

"Hey, you," shouted one of the men with a thick European accent, obviously German.

I paused as I was halfway down the ladder about to climb into our dinghy.

"Vud, you move your boat please," shouted the other one as the tender came nearer.

Fort de France harbour was not the easiest of places to anchor, partly because the holding was not good in some areas, and partly because the place was so busy, there is at least a hundred other yachts anchored in the same area.

Once anchored, you would not normally consider moving until ready to sail and certainly moving at night would have created a further hazard, which I was not going to indulge in without a very good reason.

"Why do you want us to move?" I asked, puzzled.

The two men now drew alongside, and the one driving the rather swish tender stood up. "I have been instructed by the Captain of Lady Bertha," he turned and pointed to a large motor yacht slowly approaching the harbour area, "to request all these boats to move." He swept his hand over the whole area where we and a dozen other yachts were anchored.

"You're joking," I said, in amazement.

"No, no joke, ve must dock at the port over there," he pointed to the dock where boats could pick up petrol and diesel, "und ve need to get through."

I smiled, "Even if we moved, and I have no intention of doing so, all these boats you see around us, are almost certainly empty, so us moving alone, is not going to help you, besides," I added, "there is a channel large enough for you to get through," I pointed to an area to our stern.

The man ignored what I said. "I must insist you move; the Captain wishes to come through here," he pointed his finger straight at our boat. "If you do not move, your boat may be damaged."

"Bloody cheek," said Brodie, "if you damage our boat, you'll have a writ first thing in the morning, and if your Captain can't get his gin palace through, then he'll have to anchor out until the morning when there'll be more space."

I nodded in agreement, starting the engine of our dinghy, and left them shouting after us. To be prudent, we decided to eat at a restaurant overlooking the harbour, just in case, but as I had indicated, the motor yacht had plenty of room to berth, and the Captain managed to get through the melee of yachts without hitting one.

Although it was dark, the night was clear, and Fort de France harbour is very well-lit, so we were able to watch the whole operation. What I was not to know then, was that Lady Bertha, which was owned by an African Prince, was going to cause us some considerable grief in the future.

We had a great evening eating French food, and plenty of French wine. The two St Lucian's had not joined us, as they had relatives on the island, and had gone off into the interior. They indicated that they would not return until the next day. I half wondered what Angie was going to do that night. I did not have long to wait.

We got back to the boat about midnight, and as I was tired, I decided to turn in straight away, leaving the others up on deck talking and drinking. I could hear much hilarity, as I undressed, and as the night was hot and sticky, I decided to have a quick shower. Just as had I finished drying myself in the cabin, hanging the towel on a rail provided, the cabin door opened. It was Angie, completely naked and with a mischievous smile on her face. I thought for a moment that she had entered the wrong cabin by mistake, and I was embarrassed as I too was naked. I was soon to learn differently. Angie was not only an extremely fit female, but extremely good-looking with a figure to match. She had jet-black hair, which she normally kept up, but now it fell to her waist. She advanced quickly and silently towards me, putting her arms around my neck. She then whispered that she had come to apologise for jumping off the boat that morning, which almost certainly lost us three places. Her breasts pressed against my chest and her hips closed on mine as she reached up and kissed me full on the lips.

I am not quite sure what was going through my mind at that moment, and if I could remember, I would not put it in print here. My body, however, reacted as would any male in similar circumstances, and I accepted the clinch, realising that she was fully aroused. Her kiss was very sensuous, and it was as she was drawing away, that the cabin door swung open and there was a flash, as Brodie took a picture. Angie broke away laughing, and Archibald and Philippa were standing behind Brodie. I shoved Angie roughly outside the cabin, and closed the door, locking it, while shouting abuse at the perpetrators of the joke.

I heard much merriment going on above for a while, but I got into my bunk and drifted off to sleep. I knew I would have to get hold of the film before reaching St Lucia to prevent it being shown around island until eventually, Liz would find out what had happened, The joke could easily be passed off, but the problem was the photograph would show me fully aroused with Angie clinging to my neck.

The next morning, as the official race organiser, I had a visit from three of the crew of Keep Me Young, who registered an official complaint against the crew of Lady Penelope. They charged that the crew of that boat had deliberately fouled their propeller with a line, preventing them from sailing out of St Anne's Bay. After much to-ing and fro-ing in the dinghy, I called the three-man 'rules' committee to hear their complaint, and we naturally questioned the skipper of Lady Penelope. As expected, he strongly denied any wrongdoing by either himself or his crew, and although I had seen him in the water in St Anne's with snorkelling gear on, I could not of course prove that he or his crew had tampered with Keep Me Young. In the end, we had to deny the complaint, but the skipper of Keep Me Young told me that "those bastards haven't heard the last of this," a prophecy that was to come true all too quickly.

The committee hearing took most of the morning, so I was late going out shopping. One of the things I bought while at the supermarket was a thirty-five-millimetre film, even though I had no camera with me. I was returning to the dinghy dock by taxi when I saw one of the race boats drawn up to the dock next to the motor Yacht Lady Bertha. It was all the St Lucian crew, and they were loading their boat from a large truck parked nearby. If there had been a plimsoll line, theirs would have been several inches below the water line.

In the late afternoon, we moved over to the south bay of Anse Mitan, which was a nicer anchorage than Fort de France, and moored next to Lady Penelope. The Saturday evening was a great success, the Martinique Yacht Club did us proud, the food was excellent; and there was more than an ample amount of wine, and dancing until the early hours. Some of our crews were very much the worse for wear, and I guessed rightly, that there would be a rather mixed start in the morning.

We had no incidents that night, and I firmly locked my cabin door just to make sure. The next morning the race was due to start at 10 a.m., and the Martinicans had kindly agreed

102

to set up the start line, which was to be a windward start to make things a little more difficult. The motor launch had returned to St Lucia to prepare the finish line.

Our two St Lucian crew had joined us on board just after 7 a.m. about half a day late, and because they were both noisy, it ensured we rose in good time. We noticed that some of the crew, of Lady Penelope had been diving under their boat, just to check that the threat levelled by the skipper of Keep Me Young of the previous day had not been carried out. One of the swimmers gave me the thumbs-up sign, so I assumed they had found nothing amiss. By 9.30 a.m. we were ready to move off and prepare for the start. We knew we had to be in the first three to get a place in the overall position, so the start was critical. Lady Penelope obviously had similar ideas as they were taking in their anchor rode at the same time as us.

We picked up our anchor without any problems and turned under the engine to port, intending to get free of the numerous other anchored boats before hoisting sail. It was as I was negotiating my way through them that Brodie drew my attention to Lady Penelope.

"Hey James, I think Lady Penelope has a problem with their anchor," I turned and saw their anchor rode was pointing straight down from the bow, which suggested they were over the anchor itself. There were three of the crew straining to pull the thing up. I turned our boat and motored slowly alongside.

"Problems," I shouted.

The skipper came to the rail. "Yeah, we've just stripped our windlass trying to hoist the anchor, it's fast, so we are going to have to dive on it." I nodded, Sometimes one could be hooked onto rubbish below, which made it difficult to pull it up. I remembered that while chartering I had pulled up a bicycle on my anchor in Fort de France. There was nothing we could do to help, so we turned back and headed for the start line, it was then I started to wonder whether someone had been monkeying about with their anchor. As we went through the start and turned to head out of the bay the crew of Lady Penelope were still struggling to get their anchor on deck.

I was to learn afterward that their anchor had mysteriously 'fallen' into a ten-foot hole on the seabed, and the hole had also mysteriously filled itself during the night. Of course, when the crew checked the next morning, there was nothing wrong with the underneath of Lady Penelope, and when the skipper had checked the actual anchor some hundred feet away, the chain simply disappeared into the sand which was not unusual when one had been dropped in fairly a soft seabed. Just as it must have been quite a feat to dig the hole underwater it was an equal feat to dig the anchor out, particularly, as the crew of Lady Penelope did not have breathing apparatus, which again, I was to learn later, the crew of Keep Me Young had.

After the start, we made good time to the end of the Bay and turned south to head straight for St Lucia. Apart from Lady Penelope, two other boats had not made the start, one was Aphrodite, and the other was a private yacht with a Swedish crew on board. Both were suffering too much from the previous night's activities, to wake up in time. In mid-channel, I handed the wheel over to Brodie, saying I had to go below, and I quickly dived into my cabin, got the new film, found Brodie's camera, and took out the film inserting the new one. In the darkened cabins I took the necessary shots to reach the same number indicated on the film used the indicator and went up on deck.

When no one was looking, I threw the offending film over the side. I felt a bit of a heel doing that, as Brodie had taken almost thirty-six shots of the race, but I felt a lot safer in doing so.

We arrived back in St Lucia, completing an up-wind leg into Rodney Bay, and finishing fourth. In fact, we were to finish fourth overall, which I reckoned was quite reasonable considering I had done most of the organising.

Lady Penelope arrived some five hours later, with their crew not at all in a happy frame of mind, but by then the crew of Keep Me Young had dispersed, so apart from another official complaint, which inevitably went the same way as the previous one, the matter was left at that. I did wonder if the feud would be perpetuated in future races. It was and became so bitter that we had to threaten both crews with expulsion before it was terminated.

A good time was had in the Pub that night, and, considering the hotchpotch of yachts taking part, most being amateur sailors, the race had been a great success, and was to remain on the racing calendar for some years to come. It was only after Liz and I left the island years later, that I understood the offshore yacht races started to run down, and nowadays the small amount being organised are under the auspices of the St Lucia Yacht Club, the Association having been disbanded, a shame because we had some great fun.

LAURIE GOES NUDE

CHAPTER
12

"There are three sorts of people; those who are alive, those
who are dead, and those who are at sea and
Then there is Laurie."

A Laurie story from 'Sailing on Silver' based on fact.
Note: Laurie was an ex-Vietnam veteran who had
been married 3 times. He was a rather skinny individual,
pigeon-chested with blond hair and a moustache that
drooped when he was stressed, which was most of the time.
Virtually everything he did turned out to be disastrous, and
as a skipper of a luxury yacht taking on charterers, he usually
managed to turn unsuspecting holidaymakers into nervous
wrecks or worse, belligerent psychopaths. While sometimes
charter guests could be difficult, Laurie was incapable of any
sort of people skills including patience and understanding.
Generally, he managed by his attitude, to bring out the worst
in people. He told his stories to us with total seriousness, to
him they were not at all amusing.

After the Italians had gone, I relaxed on Silver Star, a
sixty-foot yacht belonging to Sunshine Charters, which was
tied to the Sunshine dock. We knew that later; the day would
be a busy one. The new charter guests would be arriving, and
we had to provision for six of them, the most guests we'd ever
had on the yacht. Silver Star faced the lagoon, and we could
see boats coming in from the bay proper. It was just after 1
p.m. when we sighted Laurie. He didn't look in good shape.

Laurie had obtained a job as a skipper of a fifty-foot
Gulf Star at Sunshine, soon after leaving us where we lived
in Marigot Bay. He had told us that he had just been sacked
from his job as first mate on a large sailing ship.

Because we joined Sunshine later than him, he was
senior in service to us and I thought he may be peeved that
we'd received a '60-foot yacht, the pride of the fleet, before

him.

Unfortunately for Laurie, his ability to keep a cook on board for more than one charter was zero, and it was, therefore highly unlikely he'd ever be considered for one of the top jobs.

We had last met Laurie some weeks before. He had been on holiday to North America, and he proudly showed us some photographs of the vacation he'd taken in the Canadian outback. He had set up the camera to take shots of himself sitting by the campfire, in his tent, driving his jeep. He was totally alone, and the pictures seemed rather pathetic.

The Gulf Star was heading straight towards us and although some sixty feet away, we could see Laurie behind the wheel, his moustache had an even more pronounced droop than usual. The lines on the front of his boat had been set for docking, but they appeared to droop too.

Liz smiled. "I don't think Laurie is a happy bunny."

It didn't take long for the full story to unfold. Within an hour of docking, he was seated on our yacht with a large beer in his hand. He looked absolutely whacked. His light-coloured hair was matted, his T-shirt and shorts were creased and dirty and his eyes looked as though they'd not seen sleep for some time, which in fact they hadn't.

"Another shitty day in paradise?" Liz asked with a smile.

Laurie glowered and then the story spilled out.

"As you know, I was on standby, because Porky, my last no-good cook, had buggered off with that German creep from the Atlantic Clipper. A call came through to me from the charter manager on Tuesday, saying that a guy who was on holiday on the island with his wife and kid, asked if they could charter a crewed boat for three days and he asked me if I'd be interested.

"Well, the money was okay so, I said yes. What he didn't tell me at the time was, they wanted to visit Tobago Cays in the Grenadines, which as you know is almost a day and a half sail from Saint Lucia."

"You're joking" I said, in genuine amazement.

"In three days," Laurie repeated, "can you fuckin'

believe it?" He ran his hand under his nose.

"Anyway, I worked out a plan that meant if I sailed overnight on Wednesday, I could get there by about ten on Thursday. I could then get some sleep an' do the same thing on Thursday night getting 'em back in time for their 4 p.m. flight on Friday.

"They were late cumin' on board, an' I learned none of the three had sailed before. The guy was one of those fuckin' know-it-all all types and the wife was a real whiner. She didn't wanna go, and they did nothin' but yell at each other for the whole of the fuckin' trip."

They were British," he added sourly, as though that explained it.

"How about the child?" Liz asked.

Laurie stopped, took a long swig of his drink, and handed the empty glass for a refill.

"Jesus, I've come across some real bad Yank kids, but I tell you, this one really got first prize," he snatched his glass back and took another drink.

"She was about ten, I guess, and she thought I was her fuckin' gopher," he altered his voice into a squeaky rendition of the child's. "It was, 'Laurie, please do this, Laurie, please do that, Laurie, I need a drink, Laurie, I don't know how to put my life jacket on, Laurie, can you please come and wipe my. . .' I guess you've got the message," he looked at us wearily.

"We sailed about this time on Wednesday, an' I was getting into the St. Vincent channel. About 6.30 to seven, and the bitch of a mother asked when dinner would be ready.

'I naturally thought they knew that I'd no fuckin' cook and that the wife would look after the galley. I asked the guy to hold the wheel while I went below, and the bastard wasn't a bit happy to take it. I told him, it's the wheel or no fuckin' dinner, an' he could take his choice. He took the wheel an' I went down below and opened a tin of Heinz spaghetti, did some toast an' went up an' told them it was ready. The wife whined that she couldn't eat below an' couldn't we have the table set up in the cockpit," Laurie took a deep breath.

"Bear in mind, we're now in the fuckin' channel with waves running around six feet, an' the Gulf Star was well-heeled to starboard. How the idiot woman thought I could set a table in those conditions, Jesus!

"Anyhow, I brought the food up best I could, an' gave it 'em on a plate. There was quite a wind blowing, so by the time the stupid bitch got to the stuff, she complained it was cold, an' in any case, this wasn't the standard of cooking she'd been led to believe she'd get. Because she was holding the plate up whilst complainin', a sudden gust spewed most of her dinner into her cleavage." Laurie grinned at the recollection, "she then threw her plate overboard."

"The guy and kid wolfed it down as though they'd never tasted anythin' so good and maybe they hadn't. When I took over the wheel, I noticed the idiot father had changed direction and we'd spent half an hour heading for Venezuela. I shoulda' noticed the sails, of course, but I was too busy doin' the cooking."

"About five minutes went by and the kid suddenly ran down below. A few minutes later she was back and said somethin' to her mother. Her mother leaned across to me and said, "I'm awfully sorry, but Pippa has been sick in one of the cabins, the one directly below us."

"How about that," Laurie had put on a very passable English upper-class accent.

"Guess whose cabin was directly below - yea, my fuckin' cabin. It was obvious that mummy wasn't going to clear up the mess, so I handed over the wheel to the idiot father and told him if I found it off course when I came back up, I'd fuckin' sail to South America and leave 'em there."

"And had she been sick?" I asked.

"Sick, sick! I reckon she'd bin saving it up for three days or more and, of course, she wasn't sick in the heads, was she? Oh no," Laurie took another drink.

"She puked all over my berth. I cleaned up best I could, an' took the mattress up on deck to give it an airing. The fuckin' mother complained that it was smelly and would I please remove it. I did. I took it back down, took the mattress from her berth an' swapped 'em over.

"Soon after that they turned in, an' didn't show their faces 'til we were nearly at the Cays the next morning. I'd just anchored when the guy asked when breakfast would be ready. I gave 'im a fishing line an' told him to go catch his own. I was turning in. Then his fuckin' wife started to cry, so I went below and did some scrambled eggs. The woman complained they were too greasy and threw her lot overboard. From then on, we'd a real fun day with the kid. It was, 'Laurie, can you take me snorkelling, Laurie, can we go an' see the lobster fishermen, Laurie, can we do this, that, and all the rest.' The woman complained her mattress smelled of puke, so I gave her own one back. I knew I wasn't goin' to be able to use it anyway.

"It became obvious that they expected me to cook midday dinner, so I did a tuna salad and the wife said she didn't like fish. I told her to scrape it off the lettuce. She said she didn't like the Caribbean lettuce either.

"When they weren't yelling at each other, the guy just slept in the fuckin' sun, the woman read her fuckin' book under the cockpit canopy, and the kid spent her time makin' fuckin' sure I didn't sleep. Can't imagine why they wanted to go down to the fuckin' Grenadines anyway." Laurie waved to another crew who were just arriving.

"I was damn glad when the time came for us to sail, and I pulled the anchor at about 4 p.m. an' set off back. We'd only bin goin' about half 'n hour and the kid puked, down below agin', but because this time it was in her mother's cabin, the bitch went spare. I cleaned that up, but when she puked again, in the galley, I'd had enough. I went below an' got her by her shoulders, an' looked her straight in the eyes. 'I know you can't help puking. If I'd parents like yours, I'd puke too, but if you must puke, puke up on deck, understand?' I gave her a bit of a shake to make sure it went in. She promised she'd do as I asked."

Laurie stretched his legs, and I guessed the best part of the story was to come.

"In the lee of St. Vincent, I went below an' cooked a passable pasta dish, an' took it up on deck, this time in a large bowl, so it wouldn't get cold so quickly. The fuckin' mother didn't like pasta. I don't think she liked anything and come to think of it, I can't think how she'd be a bloody kid. Maybe that's why she only had one," he said, almost as an afterthought.

"As soon we hit the channel, the kid, who had bin below, rushed up the galley steps and ran straight towards me. She grabbed the binnacle an' puked, all over my front. The guy was asleep down below, so I asked the mother to get me some fresh clothes from my cabin. She told me that she wasn't a servant, an' to get them myself. I was really pissed off by this time so I jus' lashed the wheel with a piece of line an' took off all my clothes, went aft lowered a bucket into the sea, swilled myself off and went back and stood behind the wheel naked. The kid's eyes nearly ejected. The mother hurried her below n' produced some shorts and a T-shirt, which she threw at me.

"I was sailing 'em back to Vieux Fort so they'd be near the airport, and wuz thinkin' that at least I had the use of the provisions Sunshine had put on board for the charter, but about a mile off the land, the woman started takin' 'em all out of the galley an' throwing 'em overboard.

"I asked her what she was doin,' an' she said she'd paid for 'em, so she could do what she liked with 'em.

"I dropped 'em off, didn't get a tip and I've just returned. On my sail up after dropping 'em, the manager called me on the fuckin' radio, He said they'd called from the airport to say they were stopping their cheque in payment fer the trip and, as a result, I wouldn't be paid either."

THE GRASS AFFAIR

CHAPTER
13

*"If you invite someone to sail with
you, make sure you know what's in their baggage."*

> *This is a chapter from Sailing on Silver and is based
> on fact.*

How Laurie Nearly Lost It

The rest of the horticultural charter went smoothly, and the charter guests duly arrived at St. Vincent airport as planned on the following Sunday.

I stayed in Young Island overnight and planned our trip to St. Maarten, where we were due to pick up our new charter guests on the following Saturday. I decided to spend one night on the Sunshine dock to re-stock with water and diesel and then sail directly to Fort de France in Martinique the next day and stay there on a Tuesday night and all Wednesday.

Martinique was a perfect place for provisioning. French cheeses were available and good wine was cheap. The plan for Thursday was to pamper us and stop off at Iles des Saintes, just south of Guadeloupe. We would then sail directly to Philipsburg, the capital of Dutch St. Maarten on the Friday, giving ourselves just enough time to do any last-minute cleaning and repairs on the Saturday before we picked up the guests in the afternoon.

We left Young Island just before 5 a.m. on Monday morning. It was an eleven-hour sail to Rodney Bay; the conditions were perfect, and we reached the dock just after 4 p.m. in the evening.

It was the tradition among charter boat crews, that the last ones in were always invited to dinner on another yacht.

This was not only nice for the exhausted cook who had just come off charter, but it allowed everyone to get up to date with all the news and gossip, of which there was usually plenty.

When I went up to the office the next morning to see if there was any mail, there was a courier packet from the U.S.A. which intrigued me. Thinking it was a communication from Joan Hargreaves the literary agent, I quickly ripped it open with a surge of anticipation. It contained a short note, which I read with mixed feelings. It wasn't from Joan at all, but from Bill Cummings, who had written from his New York hospital bed to say that because of the prompt attention he had received his heart attack was curtailed, and he was on the mend.

The next day, Tuesday, we set off later than planned for the short four-hour sail to Martinique. Both of us realised just how much more skilled we'd become since our first sail in the O'Day, and we thoroughly enjoyed the trip. I knew that we'd not reach Fort de France before nightfall.

It was too late to book in through customs and immigration, so Liz suggested that it would be more comfortable to overnight in a bay called Anse Mitan, a bay that is opposite the city of Fort de France anchorage, but in rather nicer surroundings. We reached Diamond Rock at about 6 p.m. The trip from Diamond Rock to the opening to Fort de France Bay took us a further hour. As we passed the lush foliage of the southern end of the island on the east side, we watched the sinking sun in the west, on the port side.

"A perfect end to a perfect day," said Liz. I agreed.

Once we reached Anse Mitan, it was quite dark and we could see a multitude of lights winking in the distance, which told us that we were looking at one of the largest and most advanced cities in the Caribbean. It took us until 8 p.m. to anchor just off a large, modern hotel in the bay and because there was no moon that night, we didn't notice the boats anchored around us. Liz prepared an early supper and after drinking too much wine, we collapsed into our respective berths well before 10 p.m.

The next morning, I rose at 6.30 and went straight into the water for an early morning swim. I returned to the boat, showered, dressed, and went to buy some freshly made French croissants from the shore. As I passed by the bow of the boat next to ours, I thought something looked familiar, but didn't take too much notice of it, particularly when I saw a very attractive young girl coming towards me in a similar dinghy to mine. She had a dog with her, and the wretched animal snarled at me as the boats passed each other, but the girl gave a beaming smile. The name on the dinghy was also familiar and I guessed it belonged to the boat I'd just passed.

It wasn't until I returned with chocolate croissants and French bread, that I recognised the boat I had passed going into the shore.

As I approached Silver Star, I saw there was another boat's dinghy tied up alongside. It didn't take me long to realise that I was in for a morning's entertainment, at the very least.

Liz had risen just after me and had been doing her exercises on deck. She had just seen me disappear into the small complex by the hotel when there was a yell from the boat next to Silver Star. She stopped what she was doing and looked across, just in time to see a rather shapely young thing being pushed over the side by a blond man with his arm in a sling. She immediately recognised Laurie. A few minutes later, Laurie appeared on deck again, this time with a mass of struggling white fur in his arms. This was also deposited into the sea shortly followed by two full carrier bags of what looked like clothes.

I handed the purchases up to Liz as I manoeuvred the dinghy around the stern of Silver Star. She raised her eyebrows and inclined her head towards the cockpit, where Laurie was sitting, mournfully holding a beer in his hand.

"I think he's had another shitty day in paradise, in fact, he's had a bit of a rough time," Liz whispered.

I was shocked to see the state Laurie was in. He had a bandage around both ankles, and another one on his right hand, and his other arm was in plaster and held up in a sling.

His moustache was pointing downwards. To say he looked totally pathetic would be an understatement.

114

"What on earth happened to you," I asked, as I sat down in the open cockpit and grabbed a coffee Liz had just made for me.

Liz brought up butter and jam from the galley. There was a hint of a smile on her face. She sat beside Laurie and offered to butter some bread for him. To my annoyance, Laurie refused the bread and took both the chocolate croissants I'd bought for Liz and myself. "Do you guys really want to hear the story?" he asked gloomily his mouth full of chocolate. We both nodded enthusiastically. If we'd said no, we knew we'd have heard it anyway.

"Well, it went like this," Laurie took another swig of beer from the bottle, and I shuddered at the mixture of chocolate croissant and beer together.

"I wuz down in Bequia an' I'd dropped some fuckin' weasels off at Young Island and Jesus, was I glad to see the end of them. And this young French doll comes up to my boat, askin' if I needed a cook. Well, as you know, I've bin getting all the shitty charters lately, 'cause I didn't have one."

"What about ...?" I was about to ask where his last cook had gone, but Liz stopped me with a frown.

"Oh, that bitch, well that's another story. Anyway, this girl looked real nice and she'd real great ti..." His bandaged hand tried to illustrate something large and round. He looked at Liz. "Er, she'd a real good figure."

"I noticed," she said.

"Yea, well, as I said, she looked a real nice girl," Laurie took another swig of beer and handed the empty bottle to Liz who opened a fresh one for him.

"I asked her to come aboard, and she did, and had a look around the boat. I don't mind tellin' you, I thought, this is the woman fer me. She was obviously well educated, a bit of class," he added, "I guessed she was well travelled, and her swimsuit was real good quality, not like some of the bums I've had to put up with.

"She sat down in the cockpit, and I asked her if she could cook, and she asked had I ever come across a French woman who couldn't. Well, I hadn't come across too many French women, so of course I assumed from that she was okay in the galley.

"I asked her if she'd sailed much, and she said she was born in Le Halvar."

"Le Havre," I corrected him.

"Well, wherever, and her father owned a thirty-metre job, so I thought this one's perfect, and I took her on the spot."

"Didn't you ask her how she got to the Caribbean?" I asked.

Liz leaned forward to hear the answer.

Laurie looked a bit uncomfortable.

"Didn't think of it at the time, why should I?" He shrugged his shoulders and winced with pain, "I assumed she'd fallen out with a boyfriend or somethin'." I smiled. The Caribbean was full of young girls wanting free lifts on boats and quite prepared to give any story to get one. "Go on," I said.

"She said she'd to go back to the shore and get her things, and while she was gone, I radioed Sunshine to tell 'em I'd got a cook at last. John was pleased and said I could have a seven-day charter out of Martinique, which comes in today."

Liz looked alarmed. "But how on earth are you going to manage, with your arm in a sling?" she asked incredulously.

Laurie frowned. His moustache twitched. "I wuz hoping I might find someone before 4 o'clock this afternoon. If I can't, I'm snookered," he looked at Liz.

"You're not avail...?"

"No, she's not," I cut in.

"In that case, the charterers will jus' have to fuckin' manage with me giving 'em advice, they're only Italians anyways."

Liz took a deep breath and looked at me. I shook my head.

"We've to be in St. Maarten by Friday," I reminded her quickly. "So, I can't see how we could help."

She nodded and turned back to Laurie. "But surely, she couldn't have been so bad, wasn't it possible to keep her until the charter was over?" she asked sensibly.

Laurie shifted on his seat and clearly found it painful

to move. I couldn't understand why his bottom should be painful, but I was shortly to find out.

"Well, as I was telling you, she came back to the boat with about three bloody large cases, and" he repeated for emphasis, "a bloody dog, a dog," he repeated. "What sort of dog?" I asked, "a bloody white poodle, a vicious little bastard,"

"A miniature one, surely?"

"'Bout this high," Laurie bent down and with his free hand indicated the size of the animal from the deck.

"Oh, so it was a small one then," Liz said.

"Yea, I guess the little brute was quite small, but I told her that I couldn't take a dog on board, and she'd have to take it back." Laurie scowled as he remembered the incident.

"She said that was impossible, 'cause the fuckin' thing was in season, and she couldn't leave it. By that time all the cases were on board, and the boat that brought her had gone. I remembered I'd told John that I'd got a cook, so I told her she'd have to keep the dog in her cabin." Laurie leaned back and stared at the sky.

"She agreed, but as soon as she put it in there and closed the door, the fuckin' thing started barkin' and scratchin', She wanted to let it out, but I said no, so she left it howlin' its fuckin' head off.

"It wuz about 10 in the morning by this time, so I said I thought it would be a good idea if we sailed for Martinique to arrive with a day to spare, which would give us time to provision the boat. I took up the anchor an' she handled the wheel, did it real well too," he added. "Once we were in the lee of St. Vincent, she asked me if she could unpack her stuff, and I said she could. I told her the cabin she could sleep in, that just happened to have a communicatin' door with mine," he grimaced. "I'd some great thoughts about the night to come an' when we reached Martinique, she seemed real friendly, and very grateful I'd let her fuckin' dog stay on board.

"I don't mind tellin' you guys, I was planning a small candlelight supper with some low music and plenty of cheap French wine, and, well. . ." Laurie stopped for a minute to savour his thoughts.

"What happened," Liz asked impatiently.

Laurie looked at her and frowned, we were in the lee of St. Vincent, and I thought she was takin' a long time to unpack her gear. I was goin' to ask her what she'd been doin' all that time, but eventually, when she did arrive on deck she'd put on a very small bikini, and it sort of drove any other thoughts out of my head. Then she asked me if I minded her taking off her top. I said no of course I didn't, and the bitch did it straight in front of me, they jus' fell out like two huge melons." Laurie passed his bandaged hand across his forehead.

"She then went and sunbathed on deck, in full view. After a time, I suddenly realised that the breeze was picking up, and as I knew it shouldn't be doin' that, not in the lee anyhow. I tore my gaze away from her and found we'd been heading for fuckin' Venezuela. I got back on course, but the trip wasn't an easy one, I can tell you. I couldn't wait to reach Martinique."

"I assume you got there without incident?" Liz asked, laughing. "Oh yea, we arrived the night before last, 'bout midnight, and once we'd anchored, we found the fuckin' dog had scratched the hell out of the cabin door and shit all over the floor. I wasn't pleased, as you can imagine. I'd only recently re-varnished the interior and I was even less pleased when she said she couldn't clean the shit up, 'cause it made her feel sick. Jesus! So, I had to do it while she went up above for some air. I was just coming out of her cabin when I noticed the little bastard with its leg up against the cooker."

"I thought bitches weren't supposed to cock their legs up," I queried.

"Anyway, this one did, probably 'cause it wuz French, they're always fuckin' different. I rushed forward, to shove the nasty little bugger out of the way, with my foot. It was then the bastard savaged me."

He felt tenderly down to his ankle with his good hand and grimaced. "It then ran off up the steps and into the arms of the girl."

"Did this girl have a name?" I asked.

"Bloody right she did. I found all sorts of names for her, but the fuckin' broad was called Yvonne. I followed the dog up the steps, with its shit wrapped in a paper towel in one hand, and a bleedin' ankle. Just as I reached the top of the galley steps, the fuckin' thing leapt out of her arms and shot between my legs. I thought it was going for my fuckin' ankle, agin' so I lifted it off the step. There I was, with one hand holding the shit, one hand trying to protect my savaged ankle, and standing on one leg. The dog went straight for the fuckin' ankle it hadn't already savaged and then shot below into her cabin. I teetered on the edge fur a split second, and then followed it down, backward, all eight steps on my fuckin' arse the shit spillin' out all over me. I knew I'd really hurt myself badly, and I found I couldn't use this arm." He held up the arm in a sling. "It was too late to go to the hospital, so I decided to go the next mornin'. The problem was, I was covered in dog shit and needed a shower. I eventually managed but I hurt my arm even more in the process, and I didn't get any sleep because of the pain.

"There was no way I could carry out any other function either," Laurie looked at us sorrowfully. "I just had to sit on my tail and wait for morning. Yvonne took me to the dock in the dinghy before 8 a.m. an' I got a taxi to the hospital. It took 'em all fuckin' mornin' to do the X-rays, and then half the afternoon to put the thing in plaster. I didn't get back to the boat until after 4 p.m. When I returned, I couldn't catch her attention from the shore, so eventually, I got a lift in a small boat that was passing. By the time I got on board, I was well and truly pissed off, particularly when I saw Yvonne sunbathing on the deck again, and she hadn't even washed up the breakfast dishes. She saw I was bloody mad, so she got up and came down into the cockpit and seemed very apologetic. Well, one thing led to another, she said she wuz sorry and wuz real attentive, and soon we were getting on famously, we drank nearly a bottle of wine that I'd brought back with me, and she told me that she'd spent a year doin' aroma therapy in France. She offered to give me a healin' massage in her cabin. She said that all I'd have to do was lie on my back, and she'd do the rest."

I noticed Laurie's eyes shining at the thought.

"As we went down to the main cabin, she helped me down the galley steps and when I was at the bottom, she came up real close," Laurie breathed heavily. "Remember, she wore nothing on the top and well, I guess I got a bit overheated, and my shorts couldn't contain what was in there."

Laurie shot Liz a sly glance and seemed upset when he saw she was unimpressed.

"She noticed and helped me get my trousers off, then she gently drew me towards her cabin opened the door and told me to go in first and lie down on the berth. I could feel her breasts pushing my back, and she was holding my hips with both her hands as she steered me where she wanted me to go. I could hear her breathing heavily, and I was getting really twitched up by now."

"Are you sure you want to tell us the rest?" Liz smiled.

"Yeah, well, I'd forgotten the fuckin' dog, hadn't I? As I walked into the cabin, the bloody thing flew for the only piece of my anatomy that was stickin' out." Laurie put his good hand down carefully towards the lower part of his anatomy, a grimace of pain on his face. "Have you ever seen a lacerated pen...?"

"Strangely, no," said Liz, with an intake of breath, "and, I've no interest in seeing one now," she said firmly.

"Well, I'd to get back to fuckin' hospital, and how do you tell a nurse that a fuckin' dog bit your crotch? They thought it was very funny particularly as the bloody thing had swollen to three times its normal size, and then would you believe it, they brought in all the fuckin' medical students to have a look. I asked them if they'd never seen one before, and they answered that they'd once had a guy who'd been bitten by his over-enthusiastic mistress, but never one gnawed by a dog. They said I'd go down in their fuckin' record books. The female students seemed to be very impressed though. The only advantage was that they dealt with me more quickly this time I suppose 'cause there were no X-rays needed. I was back on the boat by 8 in the evenin'. When I finally got back on board, Yvonne seemed a bit agitated and said she'd to go ashore. Before I could say anything to her, she'd taken the fuckin' dinghy and gone with her bloody vampire dog."

"You didn't try and stop her?" Liz asked.

120

"You're joking. I could hardly walk, I'd a lacerated 'er, thing, both ankles and a fuckin' broken arm. What could I do, hold her back with my teeth?"

We both grinned at the thought, particularly as we that knew Laurie's teeth were all false, another result of his Vietnam experience.

"When she'd gone, I'd a sudden thought. I went below to her cabin and opened the door. I half expected to see her stuff gone, but it was all there. She'd one case, which she'd unpacked in her cabin and the other cases were in the cupboard. The thing that surprised me was that two of the cases appeared to be empty. I knew the stuff in her cabin wouldn't fill three, but I'd carried them all below, and I knew they were all full when she came on board. I started to feel a bit uneasy, particularly when I remembered how long she'd taken to unpack when we were in the lee of St. Vincent. I looked in drawers and other cupboards and found nothin.' I was about to give up, when some sixth bloody sense propelled me to the space underneath the galley berths, you know, where the water tanks are. I'd a feelin' I'd find grass there.

I nodded.

"I pulled up the first cushion and the wooden cover. There was nothin' to see, so I put my hand down underneath the water tank and felt something soft and when I drew it out, it looked like a transparent bag full of fuckin' flour, but it wasn't flour, I reckoned it was heroin. I felt some more and found another six when I heard this bangin' on the hull and a frog voice announcing itself.

"Marine Gendarmerie, monsieur," Laurie inhaled deeply.

"I felt like shittin' myself, I could just imagine the fuckin' conversation as I was being led away."

'So, you say monsieur that you'd a girl on the boat, but she's gone.'

'Yes.'

'You say her name was Yvonne, there are a lot of French girls with that name, Monsieur. Where does she live? I don't fuckin' know . . .

' "You get the drift?" We did.

121

Laurie looked at me, his eyes mournful.

"So, what did you do?" I asked.

"I knew the little tart had probably seen the gendarmes checking other boats, which was why she was so eager to fuck off, and she knew I'd been left with the dope, and now my fuckin' fingerprints were all over it too. I'd a faint hope that they'd just come on board to ask some cursory questions and check documents like they sometimes do, so I quickly stuffed the bags back, closed the lid and put the cushion back into place. By the time I'd done that, they were bangin' again, and I went up above, telling 'em I was injured and couldn't move quickly. That part was bloody true. It's fuckin' painful."

He looked down at his crotch.

"When I got up on deck, I knew that was the end, there were two of them in uniform, both French, with a bloody sniffer dog."

"Jesus," I said.

"Too right," said Laurie. "I knew I was in for ten years at the best, and I thought about how I'd gone to Vietnam to save the fuckin' frogs at Dien-Bien-Phu.

"Now they were going to clap me away in a Martinique jail for the rest of my fuckin' life."

I knew Laurie had been in Vietnam, but his memory of the Americans rushing to save the French didn't quite tie in with the historical facts, I didn't disabuse him.

The French were extremely harsh on drug smugglers and the penalties were severe, including the automatic confiscation of the boat and sometimes, life imprisonment.

"So, then what?" I asked as Liz fetched him a third bottle of beer.

"They came on board with this fuckin' great animal, and within seconds the dog had dragged its handler down to the main cabin, which it ignored, and from there it went straight into the cabin that Yvonne had slept in. I thought this was where the bitch had stored the rest of the stuff and when I saw the dog pawing the berth cushion, I assumed she'd stuffed it underneath, or even in the cushion itself.

"The Gendarmes took the cabin apart, literally. They

spent about an hour in there, while I was up on top. I did think of makin' a run for it but swimmin' with a broken arm in plaster was the next best way to suicide. I wasn't quite ready for that yet, but I couldn't understand why they were taking so long, eventually, I went down below and saw the dog still sniffin' the berth cushion.

"The cabin was in chaos, but it was obvious there was nothin' hidden there. The Gendarmes were very apologetic at the mess they'd made and were rough with the dog, who still didn't want to leave Yvonne's cabin. One of the guys sat down in the main cabin, right on top of where the stuff was, and inspected the boat's papers, which of course were in order, and then they left. I gave them about half an hour, then searched the boat myself and found there were ten bags of the stuff under the water tank.

"It took me over three hours to empty it all down the head. I got the empty bags, put them all in one large carrier bag, added some fishing weights, and threw the fuckin' lot over the stern.

"I was bloody exhausted after that, so I turned in, and didn't wake until this morning when I heard someone climbing on board. I knew who it was from the footsteps, and I got out on deck just as she was tying up the dinghy.

"I told her what I'd done with her stuff, and she became hysterical. I then told her to get off my boat, and she dropped her dog, which rushed back down to the cabin. She went to the side of the boat and started shoutin' that I was trying to rape her. I gave her a shove, and in she went. I then went down to the cabin eventually cornering the bloody dog. I got this for my pains." Laurie held up his bandaged hand. "I eventually got it by its fuckin' collar, whipped it up on deck, and threw it in after her. Thinking about it now, I wish I'd tied some fuckin' weights round the little bastard before throwin' it in."

"I don't think you should have done that," Liz said.

"Yeah, you're probably right. Anyhow, I reckon that gave me more pleasure than anythin' I've done for a long time. The bloody woman then shouted from the water that she'd no clothes, so I went back down to the cabin and stuffed all the gear she'd unpacked into two plastic shopping bags and went up and threw those over too. I told her that I'd take her cases to the police station, which I will, later this morning."

"But the one thing that puzzles me," said Liz, "is why didn't the sniffer dog find the stuff."

"Yea, I thought about that too," said Laurie, "an' I realised the reason when I saw the animal on the berth cushion, which is where the bloody poodle used to sleep at the girl's feet."

"So, you're saying the smell of the poodle was stronger than. . ." Liz twigged. "Of course, the poodle was in season," Laurie nodded. "Thank God it was, otherwise. . ." He made a cutting sign across his throat with his bandaged hand.

ANSE MITAN
(MARTINIQUE)

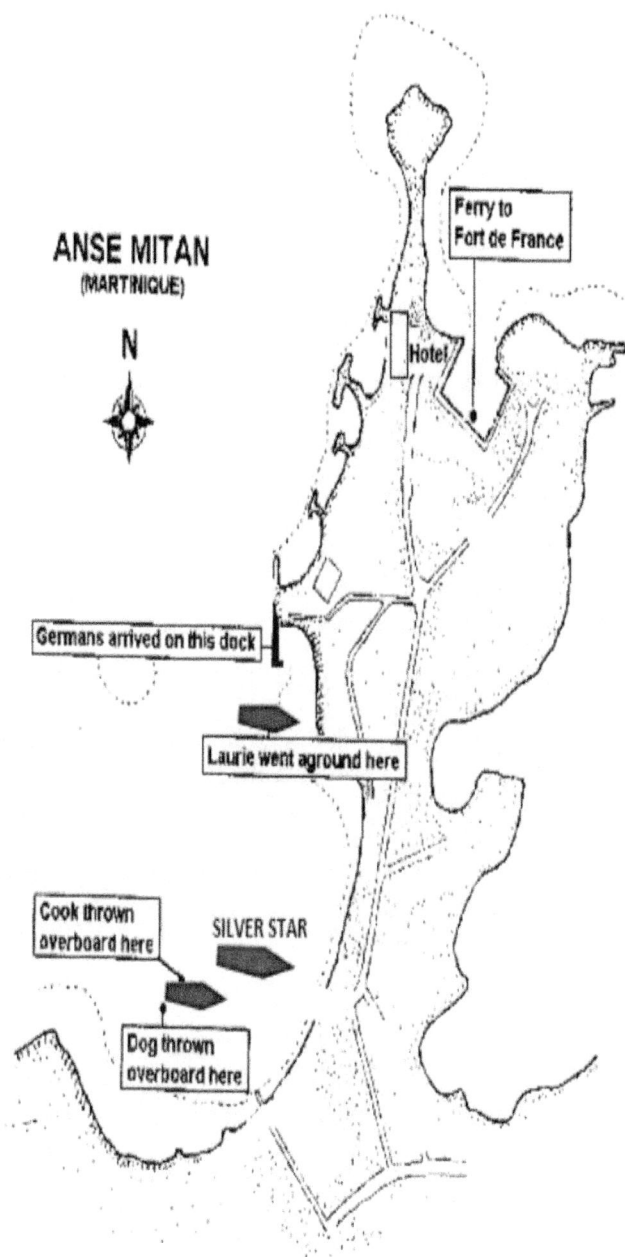

N

Ferry to
Fort de France

Hotel

Germans arrived on this dock

Laurie went aground here

Cook thrown
overboard here

SILVER STAR

Dog thrown
overboard here

CHAPTER

14

"Remember history is often written by those who don't
want you to know the truth."

| *This is a chapter from The Crowley Affair.* |

It was during the week after the wedding that I received a
call from the King's Private Secretary, Lord Stamfordham.

"Good morning, Alexander, I hope this call finds you
well?"

"Yes, thank you, my Lord, what can I do for you?"

"Can you confirm you are on your own and no one can
listen in to this conversation?"

'Yes, I'm in my own office now.'

I was puzzled by his questioning. *I remembered that
he'd started his life as Arthur Bigge but was ennobled in 1911
after being the private secretary to Queen Victoria, a post*

he took over from Sir Henry Ponsonby in 1895. His northern voice brought me back to listen to what he was saying.

"The King has requested me to contact you regarding a personal matter, and asked if you could call on him at his residence at York Cottage at Sandringham House?"

I frowned, it was most unusual for the reigning monarch to invite someone to his home, and I
wondered whether it was regarding the investments he'd made through the bank.

"Yes of course," I answered, "I assume it's something to do with his private investments?"

"No, Alexander, this is a matter of the utmost secrecy and sensitivity, and I would be obliged if you didn't tell anyone you are visiting the King."

"I see, very well, when would his Majesty like me to call?"

"I've his personal diary in front of me, and he's at home tomorrow, but that may be too early for you, as I realise you are a busy man."

"Sandringham is just north of Kings Lynn and just short of the Wash, isn't it?"

'Yes, but if you catch a train to Kings Lynn, the King's Chauffeur would meet you from the train rather than you having to drive all the way up there. The King has suggested that you could stay the night, they've plenty of room."

I'm sure he has, was my thought. 'Very well, tomorrow it is, I'll look up the train times and..."

"Oh, my dear fellow, no need to do that, I'll organise everything for you here and we'll deliver the tickets to the bank later this afternoon, and thank you, I know the King will be most grateful."

The next morning, I walked up to Kings Cross and caught the train at 12.30. I bought a Times newspaper to read and noted the date, it was 12th February 2014. It was extraordinary, here we were speeding towards to bloodiest war in history and the most interesting article in the paper was about the laying of the first stone for the Lincoln Memorial in the USA. There was also a piece about the threatened civil war in Ireland over home rule in Ulster. *Does nothing change I wondered?*

I was thinking back to what else happened in the area the train was heading for, and I remembered reading an article in 2010 where the Kings Lynn line was the first to be successfully bombed by a German Zeppelin just after World War One was declared. Four people were killed, and there was a huge protest at the Germans having bombed a civilian target. The Germans had retorted that their Zeppelin was fired on by the shore guns. Not surprising considering the Zeppelin was uninvited and carrying ordinance.

The train drew into the station and as I had slept for the last hour, I looked at my timepiece; the journey only took two and a half hours despite stopping at various stations on the way up, probably not hugely different from the time taken in 2010 and arguably a lot more comfortable. I was feeling a little sleepy as I found the King's Chauffeur waiting for me on the platform. He immediately took the bag I had with him and appeared amazed that I had only brought one suitcase.

The drive in the Rolls Royce took only twenty minutes and we were met at the main entrance of York Cottage by the butler.

A cottage it was not, the building from the front was equivalent to approximately six separate houses joined with a further six behind. Obviously dwarfed by Sandringham house nearby, it was nevertheless very large even by standards in 1914. As the butler bade me welcome another servant took my suitcase, I managed to see the part of the gardens with the lake in front of the house and I could see why the King preferred to live there rather than his other palaces. It was a scene of complete serenity.

I was shown up to my room and my suitcase was safely delivered soon afterward. I got used to the idea of someone unpacking and hanging my clothes so I left them to it as the butler asked if I would like to join the King for tea in the study. I followed him down the wide staircase and he led me to a large door in the middle of the house. He walked in, bowed, and announced, "Mr. James Alexander, sir."

The King, who had been reading the Times, got up and smiled. He was wearing a beige smoking jacket that wouldn't have been out of place in 2010. He beckoned me to a large chair near a small table and he sat opposite. "It's good of you to give up your time and I'm most grateful to you for coming up to see me so quickly."

He offered me a cigarette, and I declined saying I didn't smoke.

The nonsensical tradition that you weren't supposed to speak until spoken to, was obviously a more modern rule no doubt introduced by some senior highly paid Royal flunky, in a mistaken attempt to elevate their benefactor to a God-like figure. If it was in place in 1914, I wasn't aware of it, and wouldn't have followed it anyway.

I opened the conversation, "I have to say that I can understand why you love this place, it's so relaxing, and the gardens I could see are truly beautiful."

The King nodded, "Yes, we lived here when I was the Duke of York, you'll know of course that I wasn't brought up to be King, but when my older brother died of pneumonia, I had no choice but to accept the reins of power, such as they are, so this place is my place of tranquillity," he leaned forward smiling, "the place to which I can escape."

Just then the tea was brought in along with homemade scones with fresh strawberry jam. "I take it you drink tea James, if I may be so bold as to call you by your first name."

"Of course, your Majesty."

Before leaving the servant poured the tea and offered me a scone, which I took, as I suddenly felt hungry.

"You are an interesting man, James, I'm told you are able to foretell the future," he looked at me quizzically in half amusement.

I smiled, people wonder how I'm able to predict certain things, but logic has a great deal to do with my predictions, plus of course, keeping abreast of current world affairs."

"Churchill tells me you've foreseen a great war on the horizon. Tell me do you really think Great Britain will be involved?"

"I'm afraid so, which is why I recommended to you that you shouldn't invest in Germany or Russia."

"Yes, and I took your advice, I'm still not sure I was right to do so, I recognise there are problems between Austria and Serbia, but I can't see that being anything more than a minor political upset, the Austrians have a powerful army."

"Well sir if I'm wrong, we'll know by the first week of August of this year."

"As soon as that?" He looked surprised. 'Yes, it'll be sudden I'm afraid, catching most of us and particularly the Cabinet off guard."

"And you are saying that Germany will be implicated?"

"Yes."

"I have to say privately that I've never been happy with Willie. He's a megalomaniac of the worst type and his understanding of the geopolitical situation is virtually zero, most of his advisers are military, so it's no surprise that he may well lead all of Europe into some form of conflict, but I can't see how that ties up with an outright war, nor why Britain should be involved."

I didn't answer.

The King continued, "Nevertheless, this subject is interesting, because you are not the only one that sees into the future, and that leads me to why I've asked you to see me."

"Oh." I raised my eyebrows. I admit that what came next completely dumbfounded me.

"Have you heard of a man called Rasputin?"

"Grigori Yetimovich Rasputin the man who has some sort of hold over Princess Alix of Hesse Darmstadt," I answered. "He appears to be able to mitigate the alleged haemophilia suffered by her son Alexei Tsarevich. I understand it's probably due to the fact he can hypnotize the youngster thus easing his condition." *In 2010 I read up on my Russian history when I wrote a piece about it for a local newspaper that was producing an article about the Russian revolution. In fact, recent medical investigations suggest he more probably suffered from aplastic anaemia, a serious condition caused by damage to the bone marrow but not necessarily inherited and more likely acquired due to hepatitis or other problems. I didn't mention this fact to the King because he would not have understood it anyway.*

Now it was the King who was surprised. "you are exceptionally well-informed James; I thought his illness was supposed to be a secret."

"Well, it's obvious what condition he has because his blood doesn't clot when he's cut or bruised. If it is haemophilia, it is usually handed down from the female line and in fact, Queen Victoria was the carrier."

"Good Lord, how do you know that?"

I shrugged, not wishing to pursue that side of the conversation, so I changed course.

"I know Rasputin isn't a particularly nice person and that the Russians are understandably concerned at the influence he has over their Royal family. He makes matters worse because of his questionable lifestyle. It's known that he drinks heavily, gambles, and is known to frequent whores, not quite what one would expect of a monk."

King George shook his head in disbelief and then smiled. "Is there anything you don't know about, James?"

What I did not mention was that Rasputin was to be shot and killed by a British agent called Captain Oswald Rayner of the BMI a friend of Prince Felix Yusupov, who would be credited with the act. The stories about him being difficult to kill were all made up.

I laughed, "as I say I keep up to date on all current affairs, it's my job to do so to ensure I can advise my investors accordingly."

The King exhaled the smoke he'd inhaled from the cigarette he had in his hand and leaned forward. "Well to the problem, the predicament is that Rasputin has frightened the Tsarina with talk of a future war that Russia will lose, and he's told her they will all be murdered. She's so affected by this story that the Tsar wrote to me to ask if they could send the Tsarevich and his elder sister Anastasia to England to be in our care until the situation is clearer. I have agreed under certain conditions.

"As his first cousin, I have a responsibility and recognise that if things go badly wrong for Russia over the next few years, then it may become politically difficult for us to get the Royal family out.

"I also have another reason for agreeing and indeed this may be the real reason the Tsar has made this request; it will end the influence of this terrible man Rasputin that's doing so much damage to the crown of Russia.

"Having said all that, I don't for a moment believe that Russia will fall or that there'll be a hugely damaging conflict, simply because it wouldn't be in the interests of any the countries involved."

The King sat back in his chair, drawing on another cigarette he had just lighted, a sign of tension, I thought.

"You mention other conditions, what are they, sir?"

"In a situation where there's a collapse of Russia, the children would be brought up as any other English child, they wouldn't have a rank, and they would never be able to claim any privilege either from Russia or from England."

"So, in that case, who would bring the children up?"

'Perhaps a member of the Ponsonby family, the mother was a Lady in waiting to my Grandmother. They're discreet and would probably educate the children from their home in France, but that's not fully decided yet.'

"So, they would lose all their titles and take on the name of the surrogate?"

"Yes, it is the only way we could arrange things, otherwise, we would get heavily involved in Russian affairs, and that would not be in the interests of Great Britain."

"I understand sir, so what do you want of me, is it a question of money?"

"Good Lord no, James, I want you to fetch them from Petrograd. I trust you implicitly never to discuss this matter with anyone, and I feel the Tsarina would trust you with her children, as it will obviously be a huge wrench for her. I would go myself if I could, but of course, that would be impossible, because of the current volatile political situation."

I frowned, "Of course, but why me, you must have many trusted people you could have called on?"

"I could not ask a Royal, I could not ask anyone from the military, I had to have someone both the Tsarina and I trust, who better than the man with whom I place my money? Also, the one 'fly in the ointment,' in Germany and to have someone who has a German Baronetcy given personally by the Kaiser must be helpful should you be stopped."

Yes, I thought and someone who is expendable, but I answered, "Yes, I can't fault your logic sir," I smiled, "I understand perfectly and of course I'll do as you ask, but do you have a suggestion as to how I would get them out of Petrograd?"

"You could travel through France and Germany into Russia without any problem; indeed, the Kaiser thinks highly of you."

I shook my head, it would be too public, and the Kaiser would wonder why I was going to Russia. Also, it would be impolite for me not to call on him should I go through Germany, and if I didn't and he found out he'd feel slighted. If I were then to take the children back the same way, the Kaiser may find an excuse to hold them in Germany."

The King nodded, "Yes, you are right of course, the only other way is by sea."

"I agree, but to start taking a Royal Navy ship through the Baltic at this time could create difficulties too."

"Hmm, yes... I know, why not take my yacht?"

"You mean the Victoria and Albert, no sir that would also send the wrong message."

"No, no, I was thinking of Britannia, I could lease it to you and make the public aware that I did so, thus it would be up to you where it was sailed."

"Isn't Britannia a racing yacht sir?"

"Yes, it is, but because of my official duties this year, I've just had it re-rigged as a cruiser, in fact, she's being put in the water in Cowes as we speak."

I nodded, "I seem to remember that Britannia is over 120 feet long, so I would need a crew..."

"Absolutely, you could use my people, they're all Royal Navy of course, but I am sure we could persuade them to leave their uniforms in England. They would be totally discreet, although apart from the Captain they wouldn't be told who your two young passengers would be."

"That's fine sir, just one problem, how urgent is this matter?"

"It's obviously not life-threatening, why do you ask?"

"Only that it's February now, the North Sea isn't particularly friendly at this time of year, and bearing in mind the frailty of one of the intended passengers, may I suggest we sail toward the end of the month of May? In the meantime, I would like to meet the Captain of the vessel to assess the speed of the crossing and what we would need on board for such a trip."

"The timing is eminently sensible, and I will let the Tsar know that you've kindly agreed to make the journey, I'll ask the Captain of Britannia to see you.

"Now that's settled, how about a stronger drink?" The King leaned across and pressed a bell near the fireplace.

I met the Queen at dinner that evening and was impressed not only by her intelligence but the obvious love they had for each other. We discussed many things and I found her very well-informed and quite modern in her thinking. The meal was tasty but quite ordinary fare, I think it was partridge shot on the estate. Afterwards, we had coffee in the drawing room. I was surprised that the walls were covered in a light wallpaper quite different from the heavy drapes that typified Victoriana, the furniture was good quality, but not ostentatious. Family photographs adorned every surface and there was a blazing fire that tended to have a soporific effect, on the King in particular. After about an hour he excused himself as he said he was tired after all the talking during the day, added no doubt to the several brandies he'd consumed.

The Queen however was wide awake, and once the King had left the room, she turned to me, "Now Mr. Alexander, what is all this nonsense I hear about you coming from the future?"

I laughed, "I can't say that I've come from the future ma'am, only that I appear to remember being alive in 2010. Whether this is a fabrication of my mind, I've no idea, but certainly, things that happen in this time do appear to be coming true, I truly wish that this weren't the case."

She leaned forward, "Give me an instance of what is going to happen tomorrow."

"I'm afraid it doesn't quite happen like that, think of a situation where you were thrown back into history by one hundred years, what would you remember?

"You would remember the big things that had happened to you in your old life, and you'd remember the history you'd been taught at school, or you had picked up through reading. You wouldn't remember what your Queen did yesterday unless it created a huge story and even then, you wouldn't remember it unless it had an influence on your life."

"Yes, I see that,' she looked serious, no longer making fun of me "Therefore do you know the next most important thing to happen that you do remember?"

I had drunk a few brandies and I remembered the time I made a prediction when I met Churchill for the first time, so I was wary, and yet I had the feeling that whatever I told her would go no further.

"Yes, the Archduke Franz Ferdinand and his wife will be murdered in Sarajevo on 28th June."

Her face went white with shock, and she recoiled somewhat, perhaps thinking for a moment that it was something I had planned.

"Oh, how awful," was all she could say.

"I'm afraid it is, as it'll start a huge war of European nations that'll cost millions of lives and bring down several monarchies, including Russian, German, and Austrian."

"So that dreadful man Rasputin was correct?"

"Well, I'm not sure exactly what he said, but he certainly was right to warn the Tsarina."

"You don't think he was from the future too?"

I laughed, "I don't think so, although we do have a man called Putin who heads Russia, and he's reportedly not a very nice man either."

"you are talking now as though you were back in, when was it, 2010?"

"Yes, I do slip up sometimes, because it's as real to me as is talking to you now."

"What about the British monarchy...?"

I shook my head, "it'll thrive, but in 2010 there's a Queen, she is head of state and will in a few years exceed the reign of Victoria.

"In 2010 the Empire will have gone, the cost to Britain for the war will be horrendous both financially and in the lives of our youth, everything will change but unfortunately within thirty years from now another war, arguably caused by the one that's coming here soon, will decimate economies

136

worldwide. Britain will lose her supremacy in the world to the United States of America, but better that than to a dictatorship."

"So, my poor husband will have a lot of problems to deal with in the future..."

"Yes, but I've already told you more than I should and..."

She held her hand up, "You've been very kind, and I understand you must be tired, but one more thing, and then I'll let you get some rest, when will these horrendous affairs start?"

"Britain will declare war on Germany on 4th August this year."

"Oh, my goodness, as soon as that, is there nothing we can do to stop these events happening?"

"Well, I suppose you can suggest to our security services the danger the Archduke and his wife face, but frankly, I really don't think it'll change anything. He'll almost certainly go ahead with the visit, and even if he didn't the Austrian Empire is itching for a fight, they would find another excuse."

The Queen nodded, "I fear you are right Mr. Alexander, you must Therefore try and save Alexei and Anastasia, but one thing puzzles me."

I raised my eyebrows.

"If your mind is half in 2010, you must know from your history what happened to them."

"I know what the history books say, but that doesn't necessarily mean that's what happened."

She frowned, "I don't understand."

I took a deep breath, "I'll tell you what our history books say. When the Russian Royal family was captured and murdered by those who had taken over Russia, it was a people's revolt. However, when in my time the graves were dug up, they only found the bodies of the Tsar his wife, and three of his daughters. There was then general consternation in Russia, because if the heir to the throne was still alive or indeed, he had a family, under those circumstances, the Russian people may decide that they would prefer a monarchy based loosely on that of the United Kingdom. So, orders were given for the two children's bodies to be found, and hey presto they found them in another grave nearby. Russian scientists were brought in and confirmed that these bodies were in fact belonging to the two children, sine qua non. So, do we believe them?"

"You don't?" said the Queen hopefully.

"No, I don't, it seems odd that the Royal family were not all buried together, why would they have buried the two youngest children separately, it can't have been due to there being no room in the grave, so it obviously tends to suggest that the children weren't there, but politically they had to be declared dead."

"How horrific and yet you are right, which means that if you manage to save the children, they must never surface as members of the Russian Royal family."

"Yes, that's correct, as the King has intimated, they would be brought up as English children and be sworn never to reveal their identity. The King realises the importance of that, otherwise, it could create huge problems in the future."

"You mentioned to my husband that the haemophilia that Alexei suffers from comes via Queen Victoria, but happily, our children appear to be safe."

"Yes, haemophilia is a gene generally passed on via the female line, which is why Royals tend to suffer from the disease, it comes from intermarrying. The Jews were the first to discover this when they circumcised their male children to the extent that if the first two male children had died, they could forgo circumcision for any following children. In my day, there's a cure in the sense that a haemophiliac must take medication for the whole of their lives."

The Queen rose obviously suggesting the conversation was ended, She held her hand out and I kissed it as was the protocol at the time.

"There's just one more question I would like you to answer, my husband... and my first son?"

I knew what she wanted to know, but I was firmly resolved not to tell her how long George would live.

"It would be unfair for me to go into detail, and I can never be sure that what happened in my time will necessarily happen in this time, but I would just say this, Edward will only rule for a year but will never be crowned, it won't be illness or death that brings about his downfall. Your second son the Duke of York will take over and rule successfully, and for the final question, your husband should give up smoking, Goodnight, ma'am."

She wanted to ask more but knew I would not give her what she wanted, so she gracefully thanked me as she left the room.

The next morning, I had an early breakfast on my own and left a note thanking the Royal couple for their hospitality. I did wonder afterward if I had said too much, but I believe that our conversation that night was never revealed even to the King. I did receive a note from the Queen after the murder of the Archduke and his wife in Sarajevo. It said:

'Dear Alexander, I am forever in your debt for the information you gave me, it has prepared me for the worst that will enable me to support the King through what is clearly going to be a very difficult period.'

Soon afterward, I had a call from Captain Smith-Jones of the Royal Navy. He referred to my conversation with the King and asked if he could see me. I agreed that we should meet the next day, but because of the subject, I felt it was better that we should meet in the privacy of my office rather than over lunch.

Captain Smith-Jones was a man of about forty, straight as a ramrod but with a pleasant sense of humour. He wasn't a tall man, I would say about five foot eight, but he was well dressed and sported a tan that he certainly hadn't picked up in Britain. He was one of those men that appeared to have no grey hair whatsoever and he'd a quiet way with him, exactly the sort of man you'd be able to rely on in a difficult situation.

We got on well, as he'd travelled around the world, he had some good stories to tell and he was interested in my travels to Africa, the West Indies, and the USA.

After we were served with coffee from the Bank's new canteen, he got down to the business he'd come to see me about.

"The King has explained exactly what he wants, and you and I are to be the only ones to know the real identity of the children we're to pick up. I've hand-picked the crew of twelve men who will be sailing Britannia and I've also arranged for a distant relative of mine, who is a nurse, to accompany us as I feel that the young man may need medical attention on the trip, she'll also be party to the secret."

"That's fine," I said, "did the King mention to you the approximate date when we should sail?"

"Yes, he said that you'd suggested the end of May, and I agree that we would have the best weather conditions in the North Sea, which can be brutal at times."

I nodded, "Yes, the last thing we need is for the young man to be thrown around in rough weather."

", that's a very good point," said Smith-Jones, I'll organise some thick padding for his berth, so in case of a rough sea he can be strapped in."

"How long do you think the trip will take?" I asked.

"Well, as you know the Britannia is a gaff-rigged sail ship originally designed specifically for racing, she's been re-rigged as a cruiser, which is safer for a long sea voyage. Nevertheless, she's still a fast vessel, and I hope to maintain around fourteen knots, that's sixteen miles an hour. We're looking at about 1,864 miles give or take starting from Cowes, and assuming we can maintain say fourteen knots it'll take us five days at best, probably six to seven days if we hit the wrong wind. Have you sailed before Mr. Alexander?"

"Please call me James," I said, "Yes, as a matter of fact, I've spent two years sailing the whole of the Caribbean, but that was in a Bermuda-rigged vessel and about half the size of Britannia."

"Ah it's good you are used to the sea, I'll be very interested to hear more of your experience there, as I would very much like to do something similar when I retire. My first name is Evan by the way it comes from my Welsh heritage. It's the same as the Scottish Ian or English John.

"The Bermudan rig is faster to wind than a gaff-rigged boat but on a long voyage, the latter would probably be faster due to the sail area. Of course, you need a larger crew to handle the sails, but twelve will be fine considering we're going non-stop to Petrograd."

"Do you see any problems on the way?"

Evan grimaced, "I hear the Germans are very suspicious of private boats sailing in the Baltic and are illegally stopping and searching vessels despite the area being in International waters. The Foreign Office has complained about it of course, but it doesn't appear to have made much difference."

"Hmm, that may be a problem, There's little they can do to stop us going to Petrograd but returning with our young passengers could be disastrous, particularly if we were stopped by the same German boat or ship."

"I agree, but we could argue that they belong to the nurse and that we had picked them up from a holiday in Petrograd."

"That's if we can carry this off without their spies in Petrograd learning of the abduction, I'll give this some thought," I said.

"There's another way,' said Evan, "but it's top secret so I would have to get permission to discuss it with you."

"You mean by submarine?"

Evan Smith-Jones was surprised at that revelation. "How on earth do you know that? Even the King hasn't been apprised of our submarines slipping into the Baltic."

I laughed, "I had no idea that our submarines were in the Baltic, but it's logical that they would be."

It was a week later when I travelled down to Cowes to view the yacht. It had been cleaned and refurbished and was back in the water as the King indicated. I was immediately taken with her and just as I was studying the lines of the boat, I felt a tap on my shoulder, it was Evan Smith-Jones. "She's a beauty isn't she; would you like to go aboard?"

"I would indeed, is there a dinghy...?"

"Oh, my dear chap, we have a launch just over there," he pointed at two sailors manning quite a large tender. We walked over and Evan introduced me to the two men, both of whom were to help sail the yacht. I climbed in and we were quickly transported to the vessel. As we approached, I imagined her in full sail, what a magnificent sight that would be. The steps up onto the deck were clearly made for older visitors, not at all like the boat steps I had been used to in the Caribbean that were simply metal attachments slung over the side.

I stood on the deck and inspected the beautiful, planked woodwork that ran the full length. I noticed that the mainmast was well forward, about two-thirds from the aft of the vessel. The boom ran the full length back to the stern, suggesting a very large sail indeed although being gaff rigged it wouldn't of course reach the top of the main mast as a Bermuda rig would. Nevertheless, the sail would still be very large. Evan led the way down to the cabins. The doors appeared to be polished mahogany and the wide steps were located about thirty feet from aft. Once inside Evan showed me the lady's cabin that we had just walked over. It took up the whole width of the interior aft. It had two double beds, one on each side with a large sunken bath in the centre. From there I followed Evan and inspected the first cabin on the port side which again had a double berth with its own bathroom (called head in boat terms), I assumed correctly that was the Captain's cabin. There was a small cabin on the starboard side with a single berth and head and then the King's cabin that was about the same size as the ladies' cabin but with only one double berth, the head sporting a stand-alone bath. Coming out of there, one entered the salon, a very large area with luxurious seats adjoining all sides. This was an area where people congregated after the sail and perhaps ate or where drinks were served. It included a small galley at the far end that appeared to include a bar area. Going further forward there was another large cabin on the starboard side with a double berth and opposite, two smaller single cabins both with their own heads. Finally, in the forward part of the boat were five single berths, I'm assuming there were showers and heads, but I didn't see them. In this area were also replacement sails and there was a hatch above this area to enable the crew to get on deck without disturbing the other inhabitants aft.

It appeared that twelve people could live extremely comfortably on this yacht for a period. The interior was generally mahogany and all highly polished, it was a beautiful environment and I fully understood why George loved the craft and the selfless way in which he'd loaned it to me to save at least the younger members of his family.

When we had finished the inspection, I turned to Evan and told him I would dearly love to buy such a boat.

"Ah, I think you'll have the wait for the King to die, he'll never part with her." *I happened to know he was right, upon his death in 1936, he left an instruction the yacht should be taken out to sea and sunk, and so it was.*

"Well, I'm certainly looking forward to sailing in her."

"Me too, especially so soon after her refit, let me buy you lunch at the club house.

Despite my experience sailing yachts in my previous existence, I had always wondered why one referred to the right and left of a boat or ship as starboard and port. I asked Evan if he knew the history behind the terms.

He smiled, "Port and starboard are nautical terms for right and left and they never change as they are unambiguous references that are intendant of a mariner's orientation. They use these nautical terms to avoid confusion. When looking forward, toward the bow of the ship, port and starboard refer to the left and right sides, respectively.

"In the early days of the Vikings, before ships had rudders on their centrelines, seagoing vessels were controlled using a steering oar. Most sailors were right-handed, so the steering oar was placed over or through the right side of the stern. There may have been another reason for this and that was to prevent the rudder from being damaged when in its berth, so they always manoeuvred the left side of the boat against the quay. The Anglo-Saxon word for starboard was 'steorbord', which literally means "the side on which a vessel is steered and 'bæcbord'. This was probably referencing the fact that on larger boats the helmsman would often have to hold the steering oar with both hands, so his back would be to the left side of the ship.

"After 'bæcbord' came 'laddebord-laden' meaning 'to load' and 'board' meaning 'ship's side', referencing the side of the ship where loading and unloading were done. This gave rise to 'larboard' in the 16th century, rhyming with 'starboard', and again just meaning the side of the ship that normally faced the dock or shore. (Of course, most ships had central rudders by this time, so it was just a way of naming the side of the ship from standing at the wheel).

"Presumably, the fact that 'port' and 'larboard' first popped up around the 16th century is no coincidence. Once 'laddebord' was slurred down to 'larboard', to rhyme with 'starboard', a problem was introduced with the words sounding so similar. There was now a good chance of people mishearing which direction was given, particularly in stormy settings or in a battle or the like. As such, around the early to mid-19th century, 'port' popularly replaced 'larboard' for this reason. At first many just made the switch on their own, but by 1844 the change from 'larboard' to 'port' was made official in the British Navy and two years later in the U.S. Navy and has pretty much become ubiquitous since."

I gave some thought to our forthcoming trip and decided that to ensure its success I would need the King to produce some documents for us to carry with us. *Passports weren't yet available, in fact, it wasn't until November 1914 that the Nationality and Status Aliens Act 1914 produced what was then a form of a passport, it consisted of a single page, folded into eight and held together with a cardboard cover. It was valid for two years and included a photograph and signature, featuring a personal description, including details such as 'shape of face', 'complexion', and 'features'. The entry on this last category might read something like: 'Forehead: broad. Nose: large. Eyes: small.' Not surprisingly, some travellers found this dehumanising.* However, this wasn't available before World War 1, so I asked Evan to see me so we could plan together what sort of document we would need. My original suggestion was one set indicating that I had permission to use the Britannia for my own purposes and the second document indicating my honour given by the Kaiser and saying that Mr. James and Mrs. Alexander are travelling to Petrograd to collect their two children who have been on holiday with a distant relation. If we're stopped by a German naval ship the reference to the German honour would no doubt carry some clout.

When he called at my office, he read my dissertation.

"I'm not sure about mentioning the German honour, as it wouldn't cut much ice with the Russians, in fact, quite the reverse."

"Do you think we would be stopped by the Russians?"

"It's possible, they're as paranoid as the Germans. On the other hand, you will be the guests of the Romanovs' so should be treated as such, but they may want to make sure that we're not a band of assassins. I agree completely that you set yourself up as a married man. The nurse relative I mentioned to you would almost certainly go along with that, as she's a little younger than you so it wouldn't look in any way odd, and she's certainly old enough to have had two children because she does have two children," he smiled.

"I think we should ask the King to contact the Romanovs to indicate that you'd be arriving by George V's yacht for a private visit. This should ease the way for us to sail up the river Bolshaya Neva so we could tie up right in front of the Winter Palace. It'll probably be safer to get a tow before we get to the river in case the wind is in the wrong direction."

"So, do we need two separate letters from the King?"

"No, what I suggest is that the King simply appoints you as his personal emissary and the document shouldn't mention your German honour, simply take that with you to produce if we're boarded by the Germans."

I nodded, "In that case if we have the children on board, we would not be stopped by the Russian naval forces?"

"Correct, the problem would come if we were stopped by the Germans on the way back, particularly if it was the same German ship that stopped us going out."

"I'm beginning to think that it would be preferable to arrange for us to meet a submarine once out of the Gulf of Finland around say the uninhabited island of Gotska Sandon, just north of the island of Gotland. I realise there could be problems from depth charges..."

"From what?" Asked Evan.

"Depth charges, you know a specially designed bomb thrown over the side..."

Evan looked at me blankly and shook his head. "There's been some talk about such things, and they may be in an experimental stage," he said cautiously, "but I assure you nothing like that exists, apart from ramming or firing at a submarine when on the surface, we don't have any ordinance that can threaten a submarine once it's submerged. The biggest problem we would have is from mines, and in a restricted space such as the channel between Sweden and Denmark, mines are extremely dangerous to a submerged craft."

"Yes, I hadn't thought of that," I said, "and I suppose modern submarines can't stay submerged for too long either?"

"Correct," answered Evan, "it depends on the speed, but not more than a few hours, the area inside one is extremely cramped, not really a good environment for a future King, or Tsar," he corrected himself.

"Hmm, so the King's yacht would be the safest bet?"

"Yes, we will just have to bluff our way through."

King George duly provided the documentation we requested, and his Equerry delivered them in person to my office. He told me that there was also a personal letter contained in the sealed envelope that I should read and destroy before taking the trip. I read it after the Equerry had gone and it simply explained that he'd been in touch with the Tsar and his naval forces had been instructed to look out for us during the first week in June, which probably meant we would not be boarded by the Russians.

During May 1914, I handed the reigns over to Gerald Phipps saying I was going on a continental trip to assess the situation across the channel. The only person who knew the truth was Victoria. "Oh, do be careful James, that part of the world is dangerous."

"Yes, my darling, I know the risks we're running, but we've assessed them very carefully, and with God's help we'll be back within two weeks safe and sound. I could not deny the King's request anyway, not that I would have wanted to."

Victoria sighed, "I know, I'm just afraid of losing you, oh, and the woman you are temporally married to me trust it will be a platonic affair."

I laughed, "that I can promise you, I'll bring you back a Russian present, perhaps a Russian doll."

Victoria shrugged, "I would prefer an egg."

"Okay, I'll see if I can find a chicken..."

"As long as it's a Faberge chicken," she smiled, and I received a hug.

I reported to the yacht the next day and Evan told me that they had readied the King's cabin for me. The Ladies' cabin was given to Alice Waterford, the nurse who had agreed to sail with us. Alice was an attractive woman whose husband had been killed during the Boer War in 1901, leaving her with two young children. I soon found out that Evan and she were much closer than he'd indicated, not that it mattered if she could do the job she had been brought on board for. She was independently wealthy as were many who took up the nursing profession in those days. She was also highly educated, which made the sail much more interesting as she was well travelled, particularly in southern Africa, so we were able to swap stories.

I did notice one morning her exiting from Evan's cabin and she looked extremely embarrassed that I had seen her.

Evan told me that he'd decided to take only ten crewmen, all Royal Navy but without any sign of uniforms. Although we were travelling nonstop, which meant night sailing he thought it would be a little too crowded on the return trip. I insisted that I did my turn on the helm, usually a four-hour shift.

On Saturday we spent time purchasing stores for the trip and stowing them in various receptacles under seats and cupboards in the galley.

We set off at 08:00 hours on Sunday 31st May. The weather was fair with a south-westerly. We expected some rain, and although there was plenty of foul weather gear on board, the rain wasn't heavy enough to use it. We crept slowly out of the Solent before the full sails were hoisted. The yacht was like a racehorse, she simply took off, she was beautiful to handle, and one could feel the power as she almost glided through the water. I was at the helm when we hit the narrowest part of the channel, passing Dover to our port side. When I finished my shift, we were leaving the English Channel and heading for the North Sea.

The weather freshened somewhat, and the expert crew reduced the sail area, we stayed on a north-easterly tack for the next six hours, but then the wind changed to a north-easterly and we spent an uncomfortable period sailing close to the wind until it changed again to a westerly, which brought torrential rain. By the late evening, it became obvious that we were approaching storm conditions, so we battened down anything that moved below. Alice was decidedly queasy, so she missed her dinner, returning to the Queen's quarters. By 20.00 hours we were well into the North Sea and were struggling against gale-force winds that reduced our speed to around 10 knots, so much for the weather forecast I thought. The next morning the wind had abated somewhat and as we cleared the Netherlands, Evan changed course towards the south of Denmark but keeping well clear of the German coast. As we neared the Danish shore the wind changed again, now becoming north easterly, but we were able to tack almost due north by this time, and with the protection of the lee of the Danish land mass our speed increased to over 17 knots. I had gone to my cabin at around midnight on Monday evening, having had little sleep the previous night and despite the still choppy seas, I slept soundly, not appearing until 08.00 on Tuesday 2nd June. We made very good progress entering the Skagerrak, the sea between Demark and Norway, at around midday, and turning sharply to starboard around Skagen Head at about 14.00. Our course was now southeast passing the Coast of Byrum Island to starboard, and then the smaller island Kattegat to port, heading southeast for the narrow channel between Copenhagen and Sweden at 18.00. Evan was pleased that we had cleared the narrow channel in daylight. However, because the shipping in the area was quite heavy it took us almost three hours to pass the peninsula west of Trelleborg in Sweden. We were now entering the Baltic Sea, and we altered course. Unfortunately, the wind was now from the east so we had to tack southeast which meant that it would take us nearer to the German coast than we had planned, so instead of sailing north of the island of Bornholm, which lies south of Sweden, we were headed south leaving the island to port. This gave us a good wind, but we were now about four miles from the north German shore and before we entered the three-mile limit we changed course again to north east which would with small adjustments and assuming the wind remained constant, get us up to the Gulf of Finland when we would again change course almost due east for Petrograd.

I knew that the three-mile law was not followed by all nations. It was called the 'cannon shot law' which meant the boundary was the distance of the average cannon shot. It was not until 1989 that proper boundaries were supposedly agreed, but even then, there were and still are a few disputes. Germany at that time generally ignored any convention but did appear to stay clear of Swedish waters.

It was just 06.00 hours the next morning when Evan woke me. "we have problems,' he said, "there's a German destroyer that's been following us since about 04.00 and now they've signalled for us to hove to, what do you advise?'

"We do what they ask," I answered, "There's no way we would outrun a destroyer, and we've nothing on board that could in any way be termed contraband." I shrugged, "We can however protest as we're arguably in International waters, not that it'll do us much good to do so."

"Yes, I agree," answered Evan, "but let's not give up quite so easily," he grinned.

He signalled back that the yacht was in international waters flying a British flag and should be allowed to proceed unhindered.

The next minute a shell whizzed over the yacht landing some 50 metres in front of the bow.

"Not a bad shot," Evan exclaimed, "assuming it was sent as a warning."

He ordered the sails to be dropped, and we could see several sailors climbing into a tender, which headed toward us. Britannia was now wallowing in a lumpy sea. Ten minutes later they were alongside. They were all armed and looked extremely unfriendly. The boarding party consisted of ten sailors and one Lieutenant. Once they were on deck the Lieutenant asked who the Captain and Evan was stepped forward.

"Your papers please," he said in perfect English.

I stepped in front of Evan. "I'm in charge of this yacht Lieutenant, Your boarding of the King's yacht is a gross insult to Great Britain, and your actions will be reported as soon as I return." I put on a stern face glowering at the officer in front of me.

"I'm simply obeying orders..." *Some things in Germany clearly haven't changed I thought.*

"Is that so," I said, "and are your orders to board a yacht belonging to his majesty the King of Great Britain and," I added, "to insult the holder of the German Grand Cross invested in me by the Kaiser himself?" I presented him with the leather-covered box that contained the cross. "My name is James Alexander look at the rear of the cross." He did so, and went pale, as his men had already started to search the yacht. There was an extraordinary change in the man's demeanour, he stood to attention and saluted clicking his heels as he did so.

"My sincere apologies, Baron, we didn't realise that such an important person was on board I'll let my Captain know immediately." He curtly told the seamen to stop the search and they all left the yacht in quick time.

I said to Evan afterward, "They were quite happy to search the King's yacht, but once they knew there was a German Baron who held the Grand Cross on board, they immediately gave up, how strange." As I spoke there was a signal from the Destroyer wishing us God's speed and it turned away looking for easier prey, it had been an interesting experience and an insight into the German military mind at that stage of the early twentieth century.

Evan nodded, "it's typical, the autocracy in Germany is paramount, and the fear of insulting someone who had received a high personal honour from the Kaiser would be considered an offence against the Kaiser himself, not something a military officer could countenance."

The sails were hoisted, and the loss of time was only about two hours. On the current wind, Evan reckoned we would reach the Gulf of Finland at about 05.00 the next morning. "Which means, we should reach Petrograd by about 21.00," said Evan, "not bad for a sailing yacht."

I agreed and wondered how long it would have taken a cruise yacht in 2010, probably about the same as I thought.

When we reached the mouth of the Gulf of Finland, we were met by a Russian destroyer who signalled to us that they had been instructed to escort us to Petrograd. There was no question of anyone boarding us. We had to tack several times because of the change in wind due to the land mass on either side and we arrived there just after midnight, rather later than planned. As we reached the harbour area, we reduced sail just as a small launch came alongside and asked for our sails to be dropped completely as they would tow us to a berth opposite the Winter Palace. It was after 02:00 before we got any sleep that night, and it felt strange sleeping without the steady rocking we had all got used to.

The next morning, we rose at about 06.00 and were surprised to see two guards outside on the land. At 09:30 a carriage pulled by four horses arrived and what appeared to be the Tsar's Equerry, (*Konyushy in Russian, roughly translated it means Master of the Horse*). I was invited to travel in the carriage and took Alice with me. The view of the Winter Palace was quite breathtaking, being set in white and green. The main building on its own was huge, certainly considerably larger than Buckingham Palace, but the two wings on either side were almost as big again. The carriage drove through the centre gilded gate into the interior, where I learned the Tsar and his family had their apartments. We were met by a senior officer of the guard who I'm sure checked us for any concealed weapons, not by searching but by careful scrutiny while remaining affable and pleasant. At 11:00 we were granted an audience by the Tsar himself along with the Tsarina, who looked extremely pensive. Alice was whisked away with her to meet the children.

The furnishings were extraordinarily luxurious, everything appeared to be gilded, the walls, the furniture, which was almost certainly French, and carpets Persian. Around the walls were pictures of previous Tsars who could live in such splendour when most of their countrymen found it hard to earn enough to eat.

The Tsar himself could have been taken as a twin brother of George V but his eyes.

Tsarina's and a huge picture of the Summer Palace. It was difficult to understand how they protruded, and I recognised this, as it was well known that both he and the Tsarina were avid takers of cocaine and a concoction of other drugs.

I commented on the similarity to his cousin. "It's true," he answered in perfect English, "except that he's a little portlier than me," he laughed.

I recognised the fact that George was of a heavier build, but the facial likeness was there.

After being presented to the Tsarina, Alix of Hesse as she was known before the marriage, she excused herself, as she wanted to spend time with Alice and the children.

The Tsar took me to a room that he obviously used as an office, and we talked for several hours about the current situation in the world and many other things.

"You are very well-informed James," he called me by my first name; "I've heard that you can see into the future?"

"Ah, that's not quite true," I said, "I appear to have the knack of being right about things that are about to happen, but of course, like anyone else, I can't be sure."

He nodded, "The world situation is very grave, and I regret that war is getting closer, it's those damned Austrians and my cousin Willie who thinks he has the finest military in the world that is causing the upset to the geopolitical situation, of course, the Russian Army is huge, and his little force will be crushed if he uses it against Russia."

I stayed silent.

"Gregori Rasputin has frightened the Tsarina into believing our younger children aren't safe in the present situation, you know that my son, the heir to the throne has a health problem?"

"Yes, he is reputed to have haemophilia," I answered,

"but that's not a fatal disease providing he's careful with his movements."

"Hmm, difficult for a young boy, he's prevented from the normal things youngsters do, which makes the Tsarina unhappy for him."

"Well, you'll know that Prince Leopold, Queen Victoria's younger son has the same affliction, and he manages with it quite well." *I didn't of course tell him that he died at the age of thirty due to falling on the stairs.*

"Do you think we're doing the right thing sending our younger children to England, I would like a very honest answer?"

I nodded, "Yes sir, I do, They'll be safe there, whatever happens in Europe, and your son's condition will have the best doctors in the world, There's already some revolutionary medicine being tested in the USA, which may help."

"Well, the decision is made; the Tsarina is reconciled to the fact, and I trust my cousin above all others to do the right thing. I'm grateful to you for making this dangerous journey and I would like to give you something that indicates our gratitude for what you are doing for Russia." He stood up walked over to his desk and took a medal out of a blue box.

"It's the wish of the Tsarina and me to bestow on you the order of Vladimir it's our highest order for a civilian." He pinned it on my chest.

It came as a complete surprise; I admit I was deeply touched and thanked him for such generosity. We drank a very good brandy to celebrate, and I was shortly escorted away by the Equerry to meet the Tsarina with the children. The Tsar had a prior meeting with his military chiefs. I felt she was a sad person and torn at the idea of letting her two young children be taken, but she was strong enough to go through with her original decision.

We dined at the Palace that night, and at just after 21:00 hours we were taken by the Equerry to a carriage with windows completely blacked out. I was in the carriage first and Alice came in with the two children who were completely unrecognisable, they were dressed up in large overcoats with hoods that helped to cover their faces. On the short drive to

153

the yacht, Alice told me that the Tsarina was inconsolable at the loss of her children but her belief that it would save their lives was very strong.

The Equerry travelled with us. When we reached the yacht, he climbed out and dismissed the soldiers. When they had returned to the Palace, we could disembark and get the children out of the cold into the cabins. It had been decided that both should sleep in the second bed in the Ladies cabin along with Alice, so she could keep an eye on them.

Evan had decided to sail immediately the children were on board and had agreed with a Russian Admiral that we would be escorted by a Russian warship as far as the island of Bornholm. We were again towed by a Russian navy launch but this time through the north entrance via the River Malaya Neva past some huge fortifications at the entrance. Once in the Gulf we were released and joined by the naval destroyer.

The sails were raised and because of the wind, Evan told me we could take a more northerly course this time leaving the island of Bornholm on our port side, thus not sailing anywhere near the German coast. We had a very good time as the wind continued blowing from the northeast and that allowed us to sail quite close to the Swedish coast. As we reached the north end of Bornholm the Russian ship signalled that it was returning and wished us good luck for the return journey.

We allowed the children to come up on deck once the Russian ship had disappeared but when we were approaching Copenhagen, we sent them below but only for the period when we were passing the narrowest part of the channel. Anastasia told me neither of them had been to sea before, despite Alexei being brought up wearing a sailor's uniform. It was as if a new world was opening before them. I hadn't realised just what a restrictive life they had lived in the cocoon-like environment within the royal palaces.

From there we made good time through the Skagerrak and the North Sea which had calmed somewhat since our trip north several days before.

Two days later we arrived just off the east coast of Great Britain at about 03:00 hours where we were met by a

Royal navy launch that escorted us in to the mouth of the River Great Ouse. We dropped sails just before leaving the Wash and the navy launch towed us to a point about one and a half miles in towards Kings Lynn where there was a small jetty next to an isolated country road. It was there that Alice disembarked with the children and climbed into a carriage that had been standing by for over twenty-four hours. I understand it transported them to York House on the Sandringham Estate.

Fortunately, the sea had been kind to us, so our concerns about Alexei being thrown about in rough weather never materialised. At 05.00 hours just before dawn, we were towed back to the Wash where we put up sail and headed south for the Channel and Cowes where we arrived later that afternoon.

After thanking the crew and Evan in particular, I drove my car back to London where I stayed the night at my club. The next morning, I met Victoria and was extremely glad to see her, I promised to take her out for dinner that night to tell her the story of my adventure. I told her that I could not find a suitable egg for her but gave her the medal bestowed on me by the Tsar.

It was about two weeks later when the King's Equerry came to see me and to give me a sealed letter. The Equerry was insistent that I should destroy it after reading it. I did so in front of him.

Dear Alexander,

Thank you for the journey you took on my behalf. We returned Alice to her home after she'd left the children with us. They are now safe with someone with whom we have absolute trust and who will bring them up as normal children. Of course, Anastasia at fourteen, and Alexei at the age of eleven will have to learn that their background must be secret, and unless they eventually return to their family in Russia, they will be forever lost to their heritage. You will be interested to know that we have re-named them

155

Alexander and Anne; we thought you'd be pleased at Alexei's new name.

It was signed by *George Rex*.

The Equerry told me that they had received reports from Germany that the Kaiser was advised of the King's yacht being sailed through the Baltic and he had ordered that we should be stopped and searched on our return. Whether this was due to information received from spies in Petrograd or simply that the Kaiser was suspicious of us being in the Baltic, I'll never know. It was fortunate that the wind enabled us to steer clear of the German coast.

Discussing the situation with Victoria the evening after receiving the letter, I told her that although there were a few women who claimed to be Anastasia, none were accepted and subsequently disproved due to DNA testing. *I've often wondered since, what became of the two young children, as their secret has never been revealed. I assumed that their education must have been by tutors but that wasn't unusual for the time. In 2010 they would have been 101 and 98 respectively, and so I suspect they took their secrets to the grave.*

I was also involved with another situation at the request of the King but this time it didn't have a particularly happy ending. Prince Edward had an assignation with a rather beautiful French woman, and this caused the Royals some embarrassment. I was asked to go and persuade the Prince to return to England and he did so with some reluctance. I always felt he'd have been far better with her than with his future wife, Mrs. Simpson. After that, I got the impression that I wasn't one of his favourite people.

The bank was approached at the end of 1914 by a wealthy builder to develop a complex in south London. The scheme appeared to be a good one financially, but subsequently, I was horrified to learn that he'd bought the homes on the ground for a pittance and had ruthlessly evicted poor people from them, some families had lived in them for generations. I was appalled but it was too late for the bank to pull out, so using my own money I bought a large piece of land nearby and created small modern houses that could be rented at affordable rents. I was an admirer of George Peabody, an American philanthropist now long dead, who did much the same thing in the middle of the nineteenth century. I ensured that all those displaced were offered a good home and I instructed that any future developments must consider the social aspect.

It was in June 1914 that I was summoned to the palace to receive a knighthood. The honour wasn't for my contribution to banking or for my recommendation to cancel the Edward debt, but for my charitable works, which pleased me immensely. I realised however that I was one of the few that had earned my knighthood, and I became critical of the extensive corruption in the current society and the treatment of those not born to privilege.

My relationship with Victoria strengthened if anything and we rarely missed a weekend of being together, although we could never appear as a couple in public, which probably hurt her more than me. John had stopped coming to the bank altogether now, and in his own way, he was happy on the estate, but although the symptoms of his illness slowed probably due to less stress, it was slowly but surely killing him. I was pleased however that he and Victoria had become firm friends.

My house was to be finished by the end of the year, and I was pleased with the progress but did not realising the effect the forthcoming war would have on skilled labour.

The war started at the beginning of August and there was what I would call war fever in Britain as almost all young men were desperate to show their wives and families that they were true patriots. The thought of the excitement and glory pulled thousands of young men into the slaughter.

When I reached my office one morning, I received a handwritten note from Winston Churchill with an Admiralty seal on the envelope. I opened it and read the contents.

Dear James,

Damn you for being right. If it is as bad as you forecast, and you have always been right up to now, I fear for the British Empire and those thousands of young men who will perish in the mud. If only I could have stopped it.
I am looking out for the corporal!

Yours

Winston

Gerald came into my office the same morning and said he was joining the colours. I immediately asked him to bring Penelope to the office before he made his final decision. He agreed to do so.

The next morning, I told them my whole story, I wasn't concerned whether they believed it or not, but I told them of the horrors of this war and the complete inadequacy and incompetence of the Generals to fight a war they didn't understand.

I showed them Winston's letter, which moved both.

I turned to Gerald. "You owe a commitment to your country, and you'll not dispose of that commitment by being killed in a muddy field in Flanders. The country will need men like you when the war is over, as there'll be precious little expertise left. You also owe a commitment to Penelope and your future children and finally, you owe a commitment to the bank. We're going to have to work hard to supply the needs of Great Britain, as this war will be costly not just in lives but in money too. Now, go away and consider your position very carefully."

I stood up, and Penelope came toward me in tears, "Thank you, James, oh thank you," I told them both to go home, and that Gerald needn't return until they had the time to consider the future.

It was a very sober man who entered my office the next day. "I've decided to stay," said Gerald, "I know people will say I'm a coward, but it would be easy for me join the colours and in a sense that would be cowardly."

I nodded, "You'll see that you've made the right decision, Now I'm going to write to Winston and ask him to ensure that you are not called up because that's what will happen when they run out of bodies. I'll tell him truthfully that you are needed by the bank to help ensure that the government has a ready supply of finance to be able to win the war. He of all people will understand."

When Gerald left my office, I felt that at least I had been able to change one life for the better.

By the end of 1914, the war was proving to be disastrous, and the building of my house was now moving at a snail's pace due to the lack of labour. My personal finances were increasing in leaps and bounds, war regrettably being very profitable for those with money and not involved in the fighting. I kept my money in cash in a personal account with a secret code, that was 23234-D, which was part of my old army number, and I put this in my safe along with my list of further investments I had worked on up to 1945.

I started to think more about my Tory and how she'd have been able to manage without me in the intervening years, did she think I had abandoned her I wondered, if would she have married again, all these thoughts kept running through my mind to the extent I became rather depressed. The war news continued to be bad, which didn't help.

The bank was now running well, and I received enquiries from the new team at Byron's Bank asking if I would be interested in merging our interests, I turned them down because I guessed that if I carried out an investigation of their bank, I would find things that would destroy them, from a strict business point of view, that would have been a good business decision, but I wasn't interested in getting bigger, just better and more efficient.

The year, 1915 came and I was concentrating on the completion of my house which promised to be ready for me to move to in early May. I bought furniture and the latest equipment as well as some very expensive pictures including Monet's, Renoir's, one or two of Van Gogh's including the Harvest at La Crau and The Peach Trees in Blossom, both of which I liked, and later I added Turner's Venice. All were put in store to await my move.

Prince of Wales (George)   About 1907   Crew of yacht Britannia

Emperor of Russia's daughters with mother and sister   Emperor of Russia's only son

The little Cæsarevitch

THE PREPARATION

CHAPTER
15

"More haste, less speed, is something every sailor should heed".

This chapter was taken from 'Sailing on Silver. It was about our last sail in a charter yacht.

Prior to returning the yacht, we were sailing to the American Virgin Islands, we were moored in Philipsburg, Sint Maarten, on the Dutch side of the island, one of the Leeward chain. We had a good morning, returning with French bread from the French side, (Saint Martin) along with ripe brie and a pound of butter. We had decided to make the best of our swan song.

We took the dinghy back to the yacht, and upon approaching it, I noticed another smaller yacht had anchored very close by. It was also flying an American flag. Normally I would be irritated at a boat being so close to us, as often, if the wind changes at night, it means one's boat plays bumps a daisy with the other, not at all conducive to a good night's sleep. In this case, however, once our expected passenger was to be on board later in the day, we had decided to sail around to Marigot Bay on the French side and moor there for the night, the reason being that the anchorage is two hours nearer to the Virgin Islands and would thus reduce our sailing time the next day.

When we climbed on board, we noticed that there was a rather portly heavyset middle-aged man lounging in the other boat's cockpit. He was somewhat unshaven and was drinking beer from a can. A baseball cap was placed squarely on his head back to front. (I have often wondered since if the writers of 'The Simpsons' were around at the time because this man was the spitting image of Homer Simpson). There was also a woman who must have been his wife because I could not imagine even the most sightless of men picking her as a mistress. Neither of them looked particularly happy with life. One of the reasons was shortly to become apparent as Liz and I spread out our feast on the cockpit table. From down below on the other yacht came a nasal wail, "Mommy, I wanna go swimming." The child, who appeared to be female, emerged from the depths like some white blob.

These were bare boaters, (tourist sailors who have hired a yacht without crew).

The mother, a two-hundred-and-fifty-pound ball of obese flesh, yelled back at the 'little' girl, "no, you can't go swimmin."

"Why can't I go swimmin?" She whined.

"'Cause of ... sharks..." answered the mother, triumphantly.

I raised my eyebrows at Liz, who was just about to bite into a huge chunk of bread liberally covered with brie, she grinned.

The girl looked over the side of their boat, her blown-up butterfly wings looking like some weird alien attachment fastened to her bleached upper arms, tinged with red from unaccustomed exposure to the sun.

"There ain't no sharks," she scowled at the water, half hanging over the rail at the stern.

"Yea, there are so, real big ones. In any case, I gotta' help yer dad do the mast, so I can't watch yer..."

I had noticed the father rather laboriously getting up and going to the mast where he tied the boson's chair to the main halyard (A boson's chair is usually a fabric chair, which one straps oneself into when being hauled up the mast to carry out repairs). As they say in the television program,

Gladiators, don't try this one at home, as it could be injurious to your health.

"Hey Margo, com'n hold this rope," the big man held one end of the halyard, the other end was already hooked onto the chair which he had struggled into with great difficulty. The manufacturers never have imagined that a man of his bulk would be involved in shinning up a mast.

Margo waddled onto the upper deck and took the line.

"Now, what yer do, is yer wind it round this," he pointed to the mast winch, "and with this handle yer turn it 'til I'm up, yer got it?"

"Yea," she answered, looking worriedly up the mast, which was well over thirty-five feet high. I noticed she stepped well out of the way of his trajectory, a wise precaution in case he fell, not that I blamed her.

"Okay, I'm ready..."

She wound the line around the winch and started to turn it.

Now some well-equipped yachts are supplied with what we call self-tailing winches, this means that when the winch is turned, the spring-loaded sides ensure the line does not slip. In this case, they had no such luxury so, this meant that 'mommy' had to take the slack with one hand while turning the winch handle with the other, no mean feat in normal circumstances, but with 250 lbs or so of male flesh on the other end, the job was not easy.

Liz looked at me. "James, you must offer to help..."

I groaned, as I put down my wine glass, and went over to the side of the yacht.

"Hi," I called, "can I give you a hand?" I don't know what it is about the average American, who is normally the most polite and generous of individuals, but when asked if they need help, they appear to take it as some sort of huge effrontery to their pride.

The woman now very red-faced and showing

considerable strain, turned and glowered at me. I looked up at the man, now some ten feet off the deck.

"We don't need yer help," he almost yelped.

"Thank you," I said sarcastically, under my breath. I smiled and held my hand up. "Okay, okay," I said, and wandered back, somewhat relieved, towards my wine and French bread.

The woman, as if to prove that she could manage on her own, made an extraordinary effort, and the boson's chair rapidly moved upwards, so rapidly in fact that the unfortunate man crunched his head with some force on the bottom of the crossbar. "Yeow for Gawd's sake Margo..." He yelled down as he moved one of his hands from around the mast, to probe for the inevitable lump, that must have been forming on top of his head. His baseball cap, spun away from the boat to land with a plop in the water.

She stared up at him. "Well for fucks sake watch what yer doin', this ain't easy yer know..." She was now bathed in sweat, and her breathing was laboured. She continued turning the winch handle, but rather more slowly. He was probably quite near the top when he called down.

"Okay, Margo, jus' hold it...." He didn't finish.

At that precise moment, there was a shrill scream from the child, as she disappeared over the stern of their boat, the top half of her ample torso having been doubled over the rail had at last given way to the normal forces of nature...Gravity.

Both Liz and I jumped up and rushed to the side, but unfortunately for Bart, as we were later to learn the man up the mast was called, so did his wife.

Now, a loose line wrapped around a normal winch may slow down a weight on the other end, but not by very much. This simply meant that our fat American friend had minutely more time to consider his impending dive into the deck than he might otherwise have done.

What had happened was that Margo had simply let go

165

of her end of the line and rushed towards the side of the yacht where her child had fallen over. She got halfway there, when she heard Bart's strangled cry as he lost his grip on the mast, and the line started to slip off the winch, which had the effect of Bart plunging rapidly downwards.

Realising what she had done, she made a desperate attempt to turn and at the same time grab the fast-moving line. Unfortunately for her, she did not realise what any sailor knows, that to try to stop a line that is moving with any force or speed, is like trying to hold on to a red-hot poker. Indeed, the burn, one can get from such rash behaviour is like a burn from a red-hot poker.

Margo did manage to grab the line. and then let out a piercing scream as she immediately let go. As she did so, her weight was still transferred seawards, throwing her backwards against the rail. There was a splinter of over-stressed steel as two stanchions gave way, and Margo disappeared over the side with a huge splash, the wash from which, even rocked our yacht.

When one is at sea, it is sod's law that says any loose line will almost certainly snag on something, just when you don't want it to. The same sod's law saved Bart. The line still twisted loosely around the winch, fouled, and Bart hurtling down like some bungee jumper, came so close to the deck I thought he had hit it. I was starting to think in my mind as to how I would call the emergency services on the radio when the bloated body jumped back skywards by some three feet and hung there. A dark stain appeared in the front of his swimsuit, and I realised that apart from the embarrassment of wetting himself, Bart had been extremely lucky. The girl who had caused all the trouble was swimming quite merrily at the stern of the yacht but rapidly retreated up the aft steps when she saw her mother hurtling towards her like some out-of-control killer whale. Wisely, the girl was shot down below, as mother heaved herself up, and for the first time saw that Bart was not desperately injured.

"You, okay?" She shouted.

"No thanks to you yer fuckin' bitch, get me down,"

166

Margo glowered as she moved over to the winch, but she couldn't move the line, it was jammed solid. She disappeared below, and there was a scream and yowl, as no doubt the child was summarily chastised. Margo reappeared with a very large bread knife. Bart was still cursing and swearing as Margo just cut the line, moving rapidly out of the way, as the unfortunate Bart fell three feet to the deck with a howl of pain.

Liz and I were by now seeing the funny side of the antics on the nearby boat, and to avoid being seen laughing, we went below and watched from a glass-darkened porthole.

Within minutes, Bart was back on deck dressed in another swimsuit. He turned on the engine, picked up their anchor, and we watched for fifteen minutes as he tried to place the boat as near to his sodden but just floating baseball cap as possible, and then tried to pick it up with a boat hook. Margo who was sitting sulking in the cockpit neither helped with the steering of the boat, nor with the retrieval operation.

Hooking an object from the deck of a yacht is not as easy as it looks, and even Liz, who from time to time was used to bringing in buoys for us to tie up to, had more than once disappeared over the side when she misjudged the line she was trying to pick up.

Bart was neither experienced in steering the boat nor in using a boat hook, we were royally entertained as he gunned the engine so that the hull was near the cap, put it into neutral, grabbed the boat hook, and waddled to the side.

Of course, because he had moved the boat too fast, the force of the wake had long pushed the cap several yards away before he got to it, and so he would try again with precisely the same result.

I couldn't stand it, I reasoned that if he carried on the way he was, he would almost certainly smash into something and that something could be us. I jumped into our powerful inflatable dinghy, and within thirty seconds, I had handed the wet cap up to him.

He clearly was not happy with this unwarranted

interference, and as he snatched it from my hand, he snarled thanks, but I could've managed..."

"Sure," I smiled and gunned the engine of the inflatable back to our yacht.

I had just climed on board; when I noticed that Bart had the yacht under full engine power headed straight across our bow, heading seawards. He was so close I thought for a minute he had fouled our anchor line but thankfully, it remained intact.

"Where is he going?" I asked Liz, who had come back on deck.

She shook her head, watching the retreating trio.

"Wherever it is, he's going far too fast," I murmured under my breath.

"Presumably, he's going to another anchorage, where he can enjoy his disasters without an audience," Liz grinned.

I watched with dismay. "The idiot is headed straight for the sandbank," a well-known boat killer in the middle of the bay.

"HEY, Try Again," (the name of their yacht) I shouted.

Bart turned around and saw me gesticulating.

He then did the most extraordinary thing. He left his wheel and went to the stern of his boat, which was the nearest part to us, and he showed us his middle finger sticking up on his right arm and then jerking the same arm upwards while bringing his left hand to clasp his right bicep. I understood the message of course, but his stance was suddenly interrupted when his yacht hit the sand bank at ten knots. He achieved his second flight of the day as he was hurled at the wheel of the yacht, which bent backward with the force of his weight.

They were still stuck when we passed them some hours later when sailing to Marigot. As we went by, I gave them a cheery wave. The three of them were sitting on the side of the boat next to each other, heads on hands and looking extremely miserable. They did not wave back.

"I hope they are not waiting for the tide," said Liz smiling.

I frowned, "there is no tide in the Caribbean."

"Yes, I know that, but I wonder if they do...?"

I smiled I would definitely miss sailing I thought to myself.

THE IDEA

CHAPTER
16

"Never underestimate a woman,

Particularly if she's a spy".

> *This is the opening chapter to the 'Gorazde Incident'*
> *about the Balkans war where a female spy, with a little*
> *help, won the war for Bosnia.*

"Well, Demitri, what did you think of the London conference?" The man speaking got up from the comfortable chair behind his large metal desk and walked over to the window. He looked through the thick armoured glass down at Sarajevo Memorial square, six floors below, remembering it as it had been, bedecked with flowers, shrubs, and trees. Now it was a bombsite, literally. The roads around the square were pock-marked with shell and mortar craters. He looked up at the sky; it was blue, with barely a cloud. He noticed a puff of smoke from a far-off hill and quickly walked back to his desk.

John Petrovic looked like the senior civil servant he was. Medium height, grey swept-back hair, smart western double-breasted suit, and black polished shoes. The red tie was the only slight spot of colour allowed in the drab surroundings. He sat down, taking off his metal-rimmed glasses. John was still a good-looking man despite his nearly sixty years, his face strong and intelligent; the eyes were a piercing blue, which seemed to read one, a useful attribute for the head of the Bosnian Security Service.

170

The man slouched in the seat opposite, was unshaven and wore a crumpled suit. Demitri Orvis, a thin-faced man of indeterminate years, had been in London as an observer at the London Summit Conference on Bosnia only twenty-four hours before.

He grimaced, almost a sneer.

"It was the usual stuff, John. The USA wants to bomb the hell out of the Bosnian Serbs, at little risk to themselves, and then their pilots scuttle home before they're shot up. I suppose such an act would make good picture opportunities for American television and create an aura of bravado around the White House," he said tiredly.

"The French want the world to know that they are the only ones prepared to stand up and fight on the ground, and that will continue to be their stance until someone calls their bluff... It's good political rhetoric... for the new president."

"And the British?"

John Petrovic lit a cigarette and almost as an afterthought, offered one to Demitri who refused.

"Ah, the British, the British want a situation where they can hold their hands on their hearts and say, we are really your friends, we did our best, but... and then withdraw their troops, get out as fast as they can. In my opinion, they've no interest in getting further involved with our war," Demitri loosened his already loose tie, making him look even more untidy.

John Petrovic looked up at the peeling ceiling of his office and blew out some smoke. "You don't think they're concerned about the greater involvement then?"

"You mean the war spilling over into Macedonia or Albania...?"

John nodded.

"I think they know we're beaten, and it's just a matter of time before we must accept a humiliating defeat, one that'll give the Serbs almost complete control over our

171

future. After all, who is going to carry the war over the borders? The Bosnian Muslims? What with, pikes, spears, and pieces of wood against tanks? No John, that's why the British don't want us to be armed, with arms The conflict could easily widen, and then the powers would have to act, but without arms..." Demitri threw up his hands in the air, "we are to be sacrificed on the altar of the British..." Demitri stopped, searching for the word.

"Parsimony is the English word I believe. Do everything with care, until it is too late to act, they are experts at it," John smiled grimly. "What we need Demitri is something to polarise the West into action, some act that will so infuriate them against the Serbs, that they will have to react positively."

Demitri shrugged, "There was the killing of our civilians in the centre of Sarajevo..." Demitri knew that the shell that shocked the world was not launched from a Serb weapon.

"No, no," John Petrovic waved his hand in disdain "I mean something that gets to their very core, that hits them, not us..."

Demitri smiled. "You mean like absconding with the President of the United States..." He laughed at his own joke.

John Petrovic looked over the top of his glasses. "Or the Prime Minister of Great Britain," he was not laughing.

Demitri looked alarmed. His laugh had frozen on his face.

"You may well look shocked Demitri, but our position is desperate, really desperate. The government, our masters are looking to us to produce something, anything..., to give us an edge in a negotiated peace. Unless we can find a way to discredit Vladic and his military bullies, we are all going to be cut up on the butcher's slab." John Petrovic chopped the side of his hand through the air hitting his desk with so much force that the file tray bounced off onto the floor with all its contents.

Demitri jumped involuntarily in his chair.

"I want you to talk to your people Demitri," Petrovic's eyes narrowed, *Not a man to make your enemy, thought Demitri,* "and I expect you to be back to me with some ideas, and quickly." Demitri saw John Petrovic get up from his chair and turn away to pick up the fallen objects. He did not turn quickly enough to disguise the tears welling up in his eyes.

THE ASSASSINATION

Friday 27th February 2015

CHAPTER
17

"If you're giving away secrets.

Prepare your escape well beforehand."

> *This represents the first two chapters of Moscow Assassin.*

Boris Nemtsov a senior politician and statesman opposed to the government of Vladimir Putin, was shot and killed crossing the Bolshoy Moskvoretsky Bridge near the Kremlin. He was walking home after a meal out in the company of his Ukrainian girlfriend, Anna Durytska, who was not harmed.

As the victim lay bleeding near the domes of St. Basil's Cathedral and the Kremlin tower behind him, the message was clear: "So die all enemies of the regime."

It happened in central Moscow at 23:31 local time on 27 February 2015. An unknown assailant fired seven or eight shots; four of them hit Nemtsov in the head, heart, liver, and stomach, mortally wounding him. He died hours after appealing to the public to support a march against Russia's war in Ukraine on 8 March 2015, Russian authorities charged Anzor Gubashev and Zaur Dadaev, both originating from the Northern Caucasus, with involvement in the crime. Dadaev confessed to involvement in the murder according to

Russian authorities, but the Russian media said he later retracted his confession.

Three more suspects were arrested around the same time, but another suspect blew himself up in Grozny when Russian police surrounded his apartment block. No one believes any of the men were guilty of the crime.

At the time of the murder, all the security cameras in the area were switched off for 'maintenance'. The only video of the incident obtained from the video feed camera of TV Tsentr studio was some distance away at the time of the killing and only showed a stopped municipal vehicle blocking the camera.

Few believe that this method of concealing the perpetrators was a pure coincidence, it appears clear that the highest authorities had complete knowledge of this appalling act.

THE MURDER

16th May 2015

CHAPTER 18

The streets of Moscow were dark when Hanna Borsok was returning home from a clandestine meeting with Mary Clancy in a hotel room. She was frightened, as shortly after leaving the area of Alexeyevsky she was aware that she had picked up two followers.

They were two men in heavy overcoats and although some distance away, Hanna instinctively felt a malevolent presence. She was not far from her apartment and so she quickened her pace. Looking behind she realised that the two shadowy figures were still gaining on her and so she broke into a run.

She was relatively fit and despite her high heels, she started to pull away, as she came to a T junction she turned right into the street where she lived, but she crashed into a person coming the other way, the man she bumped into was temporarily knocked off his feet, but he recovered quickly. Hanna realised that the man's dress was like those following her, so instead of continuing past the individual, she ran in the opposite direction leaving the two followers running down the street on her left.

Now there were three people chasing her. She kicked off her shoes enabling her to run faster, and she felt the sting of the cold pavement under her feet. Despite the fact it was May, the night was bitter, and this helped her to run faster.

It was then that she heard the noise of a car coming down the road behind her at some speed. As the vehicle drew level, the car slowed down and the driver who had wound his window down called for her to open the back door and jump in. Hanna didn't know the driver, so she hesitated, as she did so, there was a burst of sub-machine gun fire from behind, Hanna was conscious for a split second as bullets entered her body, and then she knew no more. The car accelerated and took the next left turn at speed, leaving the dead woman in the middle of the road.

The followers caught up with Hanna's body and roughly searched for her clothing and the small bag she was carrying.

"Damn" said the senior man who still held the smoking sub-machine gun, 'She doesn't have anything on her.'

"Which means," said the third man, "that she has already handed the stuff over."

'Christ,' swore the one with the gun, 'the shit will really hit the fan if we don't find it.' He pulled a mobile phone from his pocket and swiftly punched in some numbers. The phone was answered, "it's Andrei here, the traitor has been dealt with, but there is nothing on her."

There were some expletives from the person on the other end. "I suggest Andrei that you find where she has left the package, or more importantly who she has given it to. I assume the traitor is dead?"

"Yes, she was getting away, so I'd no choice."

"Right, I'll arrange to get the body picked up from where you are; I've your coordinates from your phone signal. Send one of your colleagues to search her apartment and..."

One other thing,' Andrei interjected.

"Yes?"

"There was a car that tried to pick her up, we may have hit it, it was travelling fast, but we got the number."

"Okay, give it to me and I'll have it checked out."

Andrei gave the number and the phone connection clicked off.

A SMALL BOY IN CONFLICT

"In war, keep your children in sight."

CHAPTER
19

This is a true story.

The year is 1943 and the boy is four years old. He is curious and adventurous, not realising what sort of dangers he might face in a world turned upside down.

Both my parents were on their second marriage, so I came late in the day. My father was forty and my mother 36. It may be because of her age that the pregnancy did not go quite as planned, and so I was torn out of the womb after only seven months. No doubt this was the reason I was destined not to have any siblings, just a dog.

Although I was born in Leeds, my parents had moved to Whitley Bay in Northumberland, a seaside town sitting between Blyth where there was a submarine base and Newcastle upon Tyne where there were several armament factories. The proximity to these two towns was to prove uncomfortable for the inhabitants of our town.

My first break for freedom from my home came in late 1943 when I had befriended the boy next door. We were both restless to discover places further from the street where we lived and so we made a pact. Near the end of our road was another street, and then the seashore. I had seen it from the window of my father's car but never experienced walking on the sand where I knew there should be seashells, just for the picking.

My friend who was called George, named after our King, told his mother that he was going to play at our house, and I told my mother that I was going to play at George's house. Freedom at last, we both walked down the road together and eventually reached the seashore. Then we had a shock, there were large signs there with black crosses with the text in a deep red, which we couldn't read, and rolls of thick barbed wire stretched across in front of us. George, who was slightly older than me took command, and said 'it's easy, we can just wriggle under the wire to get to the beach and then look for shells." He was right, we had a little problem getting under the wire and both of us ripped our clothes, but once there we were disappointed to see that there were no shells to be found. Not one. Then I spied something, it was black and shiny with small spikes, about the size of a cricket ball. I grabbed it before George could get to it and as there were no seashells, I decided to return home with my prize. My plan was to put it under my bed, where I hid all things forbidden, such as garden snails in a box and strange-looking g stones that had attracted my attention. The hibernating hedgehog I had placed there for protection had disappeared that morning.

George's house came first, and he returned home empty-handed except for some tears in his jumper from the barbed wire. I walked on to our house creeping quietly through the back door. My mother who normally had a rest in the afternoon had got up early. Too late, I saw her coming down the stairs. She smiled and frowned as she saw my prize, it was too big to hide. 'What have you got there'? She asked. 'Oh, just something I found', I answered truthfully. Her voice changed, 'And where precisely did you find it?' 'I er, just found it lying around', I stuttered. She took it from me, 'There is sand on it,' she said, 'and your shirt is torn,' her voice was rising in alarm. My father was called, and he raced back from his office nearby and then the police arrived, followed by the bomb disposal squad of the day. I was not the flavour of the month. From then on, I was gated, and George's parents rather unfairly blamed me for the incident, which precluded us from playing together. It was some years afterward that I understood the shiny ball was an anti-personnel device, designed to blow up when trodden on by an invader. Fortunately, it was made to catch someone with a weight considerably more than mine, but had I dropped it on the road, I probably wouldn't be telling you this story now.

My enforced detention was soon turned into exile, however. We had an Anderson shelter in our garden, and as soon as the siren went, I would be woken up and taken down to the shelter where we would spend the time waiting for the All Clear. I used to watch my father stand in the garden with his binoculars trained on the Heinkel twin-engine bombers, flying directly over us. Even now, I can recognize the uneven drone of those aircraft when I hear them in war films. When all clear sounded, I would be taken back to my bedroom.

It was only a few days after the beach incident, and just after I had returned to my room when I heard a thunderous sound from above. I quickly got out of bed and rushed to the window. I saw what appeared to me to be a huge aircraft on fire as it flew only a few hundred feet from the top of our house. At that moment, my mother dived into the room and threw me to the floor. I learned later that the aircraft had not been on fire, what I saw was the red-hot bullets fired by the rear gunner from the German bomber, he was machine-gunning our houses. Shortly after this, a sea mine was dropped, presumably mistakenly, onto a house just down the road, killing several people in three houses.

It was then that my parents decided to send me to stay with my mother's sister who lived in Skipton in North

Yorkshire, an area that suffered only one bomb during the whole conflict.

My final memory of the war, excluding the lack of sweets, bananas, and oranges, which I had never had anyway, was very different. My Aunt used to go shopping to the little corner store on the Gargrave Road. On the way back from the store, I noticed soldiers being marched down the road towards Skipton. We stopped to watch the procession, and my aunt told me they were German prisoners of war. By this time, I had been thoroughly brainwashed to understand that all Germans were monsters and evil. As I looked on, I felt the gaze of the soldiers resting on me. I expected to feel their hostility, but I was shocked to feel a deep sadness in their gaze, some even had tears in their eyes. I was puzzled with this, and it was only years afterwards that I realised that the gaze contained genuine grief and it surprised me that as a young boy I was sensitive to those feelings. I knew instinctively that I had been a reminder to them of their own children and families in Germany, perhaps because this was at a time when the RAF was carrying out blanket bombing raids on German cities. It had and still has a powerful and emotional effect on me when I bring back the memory some 75 years later.

It is also a reminder, that nowadays when supposedly civilised countries go to war, it is not fought with soldiers facing each other on either side, as at Waterloo or even World War 1, it is fought more and more with deliberate attacks on civilians, affecting mainly women and children. Who started this appalling method of warfare? The same people who created concentration camps, it was us during the Boer War.

THE BLAME GAME

CHAPTER
20

Abuse is abuse, wherever it comes from.

From my Book I Am Who I Am

"There is another form of abuse that is not usually recognised."

"Oh, what is that?" asked Father Paul.

"We have talked about the abuse of children, but this is about the abuse of parents by their children, and a surprising number of parents must bear it."

"Ah, that is interesting, go on," Father Paul smiled.

"You bring your children up the best way you can, but you were not taught how to deal with them, and there was no school to advise you. Most parents try very hard to give their children the best start in life, and that often means that they must work hard to provide that."

"Yes, I understand that and more so because you fit into that category," said Father Paul.

I nodded, depending upon their life experiences, if things don't work out for them as they hoped, the 'blame game' is set in motion.

"This is not a matter of only poor families trying to better their children's lot, often children brought up in a rich environment have more complaints than do others.

"It can appear at any age, but often shows itself later in life. The child who has grown up but could not sustain a proper or loving relationship, thus arriving in later years, say 40 to 50, without a partner or the same partner. The child who has grown up married and had children and has been well and truly involved in the job of running a family. Suddenly her children are grown and are leaving home, either to get married or work in another area. She realises there is a vacuum. Her husband works but does not get home until late in the evening. At weekends when he used to do things with the kids, he now either continues to work or plays sports away from home. She feels that she no longer has a role in life.

"The man who has had a series of unhappy relationships and still cannot get his personal life together. All these people fear for the future and wonder if their life has been in vain. So, what do they do? They put the blame onto their parents who almost certainly made mistakes in some of the aspects of bringing them up. It may be that to send them to good schools they sacrificed their time working hard, which inevitably gave them less time to spend with them. It may be that they sent them away to school when they would have been happier at home. It may be that the children did not feel that either parent gave them enough love. Sometimes there is jealousy regarding the fact that certain parents are devoted to each other, and the children feel closed out.

"Whatever the case, they grow up with a grudge, which while controlled in their earlier years, surfaces as they get older. The parent or parents are always the easiest people to blame, as they invariably have a guilt complex regarding their children, and that is because they know that given their time again, they may have done things differently.

"Most parents feel guilty, about some aspect of their children's upbringing, and this is the nerve that is easily tapped into for the getting of attention, and this is where abuse can follow. It can reach such proportions that it affects the parent's stability or even their marriage at a time when they should be enjoying their life.

"So, the grown-up children are now blaming their problems, on perceived or sometimes real instances, arising from their childhood. But those problems surface because they are unhappy. If they were happy, the childhood problems would not surface as a wholly negative experience. It is a question of balance.

"It may be that they have a real fear in looking at themselves and finding out what is really causing the unhappiness. The true reason may well be much nearer to their own home than they would care to admit. Of course, problems from childhood can be damaging, but only if you let them damage you. Whatever the case, your childhood has gone, and if it was not happy, for whatever reason, the unhappiness you are now feeling cannot be due to your childhood alone, because that has passed. You will not gain happiness by going through life blaming your parents or others, you will simply drive a wedge between them and you, when it is often precisely the opposite that you want to achieve. You should isolate your unhappiness and find out why you are unhappy now, and you may surprise yourself, particularly if you fully understand that it cannot be attributed to something that happened years ago, it is never too late to change the direction of your life.

"There are various groups who sometimes, for a sum of money will be quickly on your doorstep to persuade you that your problems stem from your childhood. At the same time, they appear to offer an answer to your problems, and they give you the attention that you perhaps craved from your parents. However well-meaning some of these people are, it can be very damaging because it does not necessarily deal with the real problem and that is if you blame others for your unhappiness, you will never be happy with yourself.

"Remember what we discussed earlier, we all have choices in life, don't blame others for the choices you have made."

"That must be true," said Father Paul, "and I know of many people whose life is stunted because they are essentially living in the past."

CHAPTER
21

Some meetings can bring unforeseen.

consequences

A TRUE STORY

We had a great friend, who we met in the West Indies when we lived there. We'll call him John, for the sake of giving him a name. He was the unofficial representative to the Royal family in the area, but his past was even more interesting. John had been the senior British Commissioner in Kenya during the Mau Mau crisis. He was responsible for the whole of northern Kenya, so not only did he have to contend with local unrest, but Kenya was at that time at war with Somalia in the north. His headquarters was in a sparsely inhabited area where he controlled all the security forces, including the army and police.

At the location where he was stationed, they had a yacht club called Wajir. This club was many miles from the sea and located in the middle of a dry and isolated desert. Their main transport was a camel.

Every so often, the top brass from the UK would arrive at the small airport, which was part of the complex. This visit was headed by the then British War Minister, John Profumo, who was the Minister for war in the Macmillan government. After John had finished his private meeting with Profumo, they retired to the yacht club. After a few drinks, Profumo noticed a calendar on the wall with pictures of scantily clothed girls. He flipped through the various months and came to October. He wrote on it, 'This one is mine' and signed it. The picture was one of Christine Keeler. The next month the world press arrived to assess the current situation regarding the Mau and the Somalian war. After a presentation, they were all entertained in the Wajir yacht club, and then boarded their aircraft, to fly back to Nairobi. Shortly after they had gone, John was informed that the calendar was missing from the yacht club wall. He immediately radioed the aircraft and told the pilot that he should ask his passengers to release it and for him to return it to the club on his next visit. The scandal over the Profumo affair was hotting up in the UK and John was determined that the press should not be allowed to steal what could be a compromising document, particularly so, as Profumo had made a statement to Parliament denying any involvement with Christine Keeler.

The co-pilot radioed John back, saying that he had made an announcement in the cabin, and all the members of the press swore that they had not seen the calendar.

John, who by then had consumed a fair amount of alcohol, and despite the furore he knew his next action would cause, ordered the pilot to return to Wajir. At first the pilot refused, and so John told him that his flight plan had been cancelled, and he would be arrested in Nairobi for disobeying a direct order, as the plane was still under his jurisdiction.

The threat of losing his air licence left the pilot with no choice, and he turned the aircraft around and landed back at Wajir. As it landed, John surrounded the plane with armed army personnel and then boarded it.

All the press were furious, but John told them that one of the members of the press had the calendar and unless it was given up, all would be arrested and searched, including the aircraft itself. He was pretty sure that it was the man from the Mirror but was extremely surprised when the senior journalist from the Times admitted that he had taken it for a joke. The fury from the press corps was then thankfully directed at the thief.

Once John had received the calendar, he allowed the plane to take off, and he returned to the yacht club, where he disposed of the evidence in a small fire, whilst drinking a large brandy.

POETRY?

"All bad poetry springs from genuine feeling," wrote Oscar Wilde.

CHAPTER
22

| *This represents my first attempt at poetry.* |

OLD AGE

They say old age is a state of mind,

You notice it when people start being kind.

When you go out to walk, visit or play.

You're told, it's okay dearie, you don't have to pay.

When you travel to places far and wide, the seat on the bus is given up, without a fuss.

When the sex drive chills

You are saved by pills.

Soon your hearing goes, and after many years.

The aid you're gifted blows your ears.

The eyes are next, and glasses are given.

So, you can read text, while being driven

Then the white stick comes, and the dog arrives.

To ensure one continues to survive.

Hang on a minute, I'm not old, I throw away all the aids,

I'll be fine, I'm sure, I will be for many decades.

and then, out walking, I'm hit by a car.

which has the effect of throwing me far?

My injuries are so severe.

That I pass on within the year

My 3 children arrive with sad faces.

And then they argue over my places

They fight and fight over assets left.

Not at all in any way bereft,

The youngest one produces a gun.

And then there is only one.

But all the goods were charged to another,

A poor Indian, who became my blood brother.

Had my children been in touch before

they might have known, what I had done in Bangalore.

LIFE

Like life, what looks attractive may not turn out to be so, difficulties may frustrate you, you may risk everything in your search for contentment and happiness and you probably won't find it. Nevertheless, those who don't look and strive for their goals may miss an experience that strengthens and enlightens their future. It is what life is all about.

FORGIVENESS

Forgiveness of an accused abuser is sublime.
But there are those who continue to be malign.
They can never accept an apology, regret, or sign.
Who suffers most, the abuser or the accuser?
Is it the accuser who then becomes the abuser?
Who searches for retribution and vengeance to undermine?
Whereas the accused has no choice but to move on with time.

WISDOM

"The gift of intelligence leads to curiosity.

and then to ambition and success

But success is an empty prophecy,

Only from mistakes and failures do you progress.

and when old age overtakes you, and you stop blaming others,

Then, and only then, can you claim wisdom, - more or less".

RE-BIRTH

The exuberance of youth and ambition

This leads quickly to mid-life crisis and attrition.

The hair goes grey, the stomach bulges.

All caused by gross over indulges.

The pension comes, never enough.

And life becomes so very tough.

At last, comes the reaper, to whisk you away, hooray, hooray.

until you find the golden future promised, was all hearsay.

191

As you frown and gnash your teeth, you realise that all is not as said.

And all the money you gave to God, was in fact spent by the randy young priest, in bed.

Finally comes the great surprise, as you tumble back to earth.

Just to find, yes, you've guessed it, a rebirth,

Oh no, not again do I hear you cry,

Completely misunderstood, by those standing by.

MARRIAGE

The union of the two is sublime.

Particularly when sex is a major pastime,

Day, or night, and even bedtime

On the table, with lots of wine,

As one enjoys the divine

And then the kids arrive at last,

And sex becomes something of the past

The mother has headaches, and the father is tired.

Not able to carry out what is required.

So, enter the new partner offering more.

They appear to be mature, and not at all a bore.

But all this soon flies away, and both are left with an affray.

Trust is gone, and bitterness grows.

Until one says, it was all my fault that you did stray,

I forgive you anyway.

In the future both learn the lesson, that to forgive is the only way.

To ensure their love continues come what may.

I WONDER WHY

I wonder why I see trees in the park.

but I cannot see Noah's ark.

Is the past just a story - about the perceived worlds glory?

I wonder why there are stars in the sky.

But I cannot touch them, although I try.

I wonder.

It appears I enter this world alone.

And I am told I leave it, on my own.

Does it mean the whole of mankind?

Is it just an imagination, of my mind?

I wonder.

It appears that time moves at a pace.

But we know it is an illusion, lost in space.

I know that nothing I see is real.

Not even how I may feel.

The sun, the moon, the universe

Is it just an image for me to see?

But does that mean that there is only me?

I wonder.

Is life a film, from deep within?

Nothing real but empty skin

I am conscious of others all around

But are they just, pictures and background?

I wonder.

I hear all sorts of sounds through my ears.

And when I am sad, I am moved to tears.

But are they just a reflection, of my fears?

I wonder.

When we go, do we discover immortality?

Only to return to another virtual reality

Or will I know the secrets of life?

Full of difficulties, problems, and strife

Or will I just sleep away my time?

Until I come back to another mountain to climb

I wonder.

Because I know I am made from space

And space is nothing for me to see.

I could just as easily be a bee.

I could buzz around all the flowers.

Instead of conversing with the powers

Would I be happy and contented?

No, more likely totally demented.

So, I'll stay as I appear to be, until I die.

I suppose I could come back, as a pork pie

There are stranger things to be.

But then I couldn't hear, see, or feel.

And could disappear after the first meal.

So, I'll accept what I am, until I go.

Perhaps I'll return, as a buffalo

I wonder why.

THE FUTURE?

We scribes' of the world should agree.

That writing about rabbits, flowers

And autumn leaves are very nice to see.

We are lucky to live where we are.

And still able to buy our daily brie.

But compared with the country we live in

The world is a dangerous place to be.

Just a short distance from our land

Young children are being abused, starved, and dying in the sand.

Whether it be in Syria, Afghanistan, or elsewhere.

People are suffering from a terrible life.

Without any support for their unremitting strife

Human care is no longer there, because.

We choose to ignore their plight; it is out of sight.

And yet we believe that such horrors.

Could not affect us, we are safe and sure until one day in the future our

life is changed.

And we must endure, complacency is no more.

We believe such things are for others.

But beware, just as fatal illness strikes.

We may well lose our cosy living and all our rights.

Destined to live without a care - and complain if we dare.

Only to be tortured and to be made aware.

We must comply with those who rule

Only those who are cruel.

We who lived years ago remember the decent Germans, not only Jews,

Who lost their freedoms and their lives?

Because they thought that they would survive

Use your vote with the utmost care.

Only give power to those you trust.

Not to those that will ensure we go bust.

Some politicians wish to end our defence.

And leave us open to the consequence.

- For others to strike, like a snake, if we are not awake

Carefully watch the party who wins the vote.

To make sure they are fair and just and follow what they wrote.

Let us therefore write our story to bring the terrible things that we can see.

to all our readers far and wide to make sure that we can close the unfair

divide

POWER CUT

"Without light, we cannot see -
Without power, we do not exist".

CHAPTER
23

> This story is about a
> cataclysmic ending to our existence.

I have in the past indicated the danger we face from a power cut if one of our enemies managed to cut or **destroy** our power supplies by digital hacking. We know from the way the Americans destroyed Iran's centrifuges, that hacking is quite capable of destroying equipment as well as shutting it down. We sometimes forget just how dependent we are now on our power sources, mainly electricity.

But I hear you say, I'm okay because I have gas. This won't help you. The natural gas feeding your house gets its compression from higher-pressure "transmission" gas lines. Natural gas has pressure coming straight out of the wellhead, but it needs help to get to its end destination, your house. The gas is piped from these lines through "regulator stations", belonging to your natural gas provider, which steps down the pressure to the lines going to your home. At your meter is another regulator that also may step down pressure. This is organised by **electricity**. So, if there is no **electricity**, there would be no **gas**. Conversely, if there is no gas, there is no electricity as most large generators nowadays are run by **gas** turbines.

So, what else happens without power? Your car would run for a while if you had filled it up, but once empty, your petrol station would not be able to pump petrol or diesel into your vehicle. This means that trucks delivering food to supermarkets would not be able to do so either. In any case, the drivers of the trucks would be incapable of driving to work. Some could use bicycles, but this would be little help without fuel for the availability of the vehicles ready to drive.

The supermarkets would very quickly run out of products, and all their frozen food would be uneatable within 48/72 hours. Your homes would be without heat, and in the middle of winter, many old people would die.

Hospitals have generators, but they would cease to work without fuel. Some may last for 3 days or so, but more people would die. Pharmaceuticals could not be delivered, thus people reliant on medicine would suffer.

Dams are controlled by electricity, without power, they would not be able to control the water supply, thus floods could cover a large part of the country. Water would also be unavailable without power. Sewerage would build up, flooding streets, and causing untold misery and diseases.

So, assume we have a power failure that lasts more than four days, what preventative action should you take to continue to live?

You could catch water in buckets from the sky, assuming it rained of course. You may have a garden with vegetables, but they wouldn't last long when others were aware of them. Those houses with solar panels are usually tied to the electric grid, so they would be useless in a down situation. The same with wind turbines, they could produce electricity, but as they run through generator plants, their electricity cannot be utilised.

To be totally safe, we need the government to Increase sustainable energy sources by a factor of 300%

To use an old Scout term:

BE PREPARED.

1.   Keep a stock of tinned food in your larders to last you for at least 21 days

2.   Keep a substantial amount of bottled water to sustain you for at least 21 days

3.   Keep paraffin heaters with enough fuel outside your abode to last for 21 days.

4.   If possible, keep a generator linked up to your power supply with fuel kept outside.

5.   Buy candles and matches. If you have a fireplace, buy wood for burning.

6.   Buy a bicycle and keep at least a month's supply of medication.

7.   Buy a radio that works on batteries. Listen in to the news. Keep cash under your bed.

8.   If you have a garden, grow vegetables, not flowers.

9.   Keep your doors and windows secure, consider buying a fierce dog.

10. Trap water outside, which could be used to flush lavatories.

11. There would be no telephones, so keep in close contact with friendly neighbours.

12. **Buy James Dalby, Richard Small, and Jim Jackson books to read during the crisis**.

If you can last for a period exceeding 3 weeks, you may survive, especially if your house is on high ground.

Remember, people who lived 150 years ago, had none of the luxuries we take for granted, and yet they managed. Of course, most died around the age of forty...

Welcome to the new world.

THE PARTY

"Reality is an illusion brought about by the absence of alcohol,"

CHAPTER
24

This is a true story.

It was several years ago when we were invited to a party in Kent. It was a great party except I was still at the age where I could not properly control the amount I drank. At the end of the evening, I was out for the count. I vaguely remember being half-carried outside, and I assumed that my wife would be driving us home.

It was in the middle of the morning that I awoke completely unaware of where I was. I was horrified to feel a woman asleep by my side. She had a nightdress on that did not belong to my wife. Having an urgent call to nature, I crawled out of the strange bed, and still on all fours I felt around the wall trying to find a door to a bathroom. I couldn't find a door, and the room appeared to be completely round. It took some minutes to find the door, which I opened when I was confronted with a huge beast breathing heavily in my face. I was still on my hands and knees, but this thing was substantially taller than me. I realised that I was in hell. I couldn't go any further but didn't want to go back to bed with the strange woman. It was pitch black, and there were no windows to be seen, so I quickly shut the door and spent the rest of the night freezing on the cold tiles which covered the floor.

It was in the morning that I was awakened by my wife, Elizabeth and after rushing to the bathroom, I learned what had happened. Some people at the party had taken pity on my wife, and I had been carried back to their house, which turned out to be a converted oast house. Their spare bedroom had no windows or carpet on the floor. Elizabeth had been loaned a nightdress, as of course we were not planning to stay anywhere overnight, and the beast was a large Great Dane belonging to the owners of the house.

I have never overindulged in excess alcohol, since that day some 56 years ago, but I now know what hell looks like.

THE BRIEFCASE

"Not everything you are told or read is true.
Only the victor writes history".

CHAPTER
25

---

*This story is fiction except for the content regarding the
Battle of Britain and Dunkirk*

It was when I was digging a patch in the kitchen garden to plant Brussels sprouts, that my spade hit a soft object, I carefully scraped away the earth and was surprised to find an old army briefcase. Lifting it out of the hole carefully. I opened the rusty catch and inside was a waterproof covering containing three pages of text.

I took my find down to the house spread the sheets of paper out on the dining room table and read the contents. It was stamped in red, TOP SECRET.

Subject: 1. The Evacuation of Dunkirk from 26th May to 4th June 1940.

2. The battle of Britain from 8th August 1940 to 31st October 1940

IT READ:

The evacuation of Dunkirk has been glamorised out of all proportion. Reports of relentless bombing and shelling were sheer nonsense. I walked along the beaches on several occasions, and I never saw a corpse... There was very little shelling. The weather was atrocious and not suited to flying; the Luftwaffe sent only a few planes to harass the evacuees on the 27th of May the afternoon of the 29th of May and the 1st of June. It was untrue that the that the enemy had superior forces. The BEF enjoyed both a superiority of numbers and equipment.

It is not true that we were betrayed by the French and Belgians, it was the other way around. We were outthought and outfought at every turn.

Our government gave firm commitments to the French and Belgian forces, that we were committed to stand firm, but at the same time, we were quietly ordered to start moving towards Dunkirk, sucker-punching the Belgians to delay the German army while we made a run for the beach. The much-maligned Belgians held the Germans for 5 days, unaware they were simply covering the fast-retreating British.

Code named Operation Dynamo, the evacuation began on 26th May, and within 9 days we managed to bring back 340,000 men.

General Gort, was ordered to conceal the truth of our retreat from both the Belgians and the French, leaving them to face the enemy alone. When the French realised what was happening, they also headed for the beaches where we evacuated 40,000 of their troops.

What of the evacuation itself? The story that hundreds of tweed-clad civilians with boats crossed the channel with Thermos flasks, was a complete lie. The public was not informed that the evacuation was underway, until June 1st thus it was some 6 days after, the civilian craft were pressed into service. The vast majority were manned by naval personnel and the owners, instead of impromptu heroism, often demanded compensation for vessels lost.

It is accepted that some civilians did cross in small boats during the last 3 days, but they were only used to ferry troops from the shore to larger craft.

> We know from deciphered reports, that the reason for the halt of the German advance, was not due to divine intervention or to Hitler leaving the British forces intact, to use in peace negotiations. The order to halt did not come from Hitler either but from General von Rundstedt.

Panzer General Heinz Guderian visited his leading units afterward on the approaches to Dunkirk and concluded that von Rundstedt had been right: only 50% of the German tanks were still in battle condition, supply lines were stretched to breaking point and any further advance across the reclaimed but still treacherous wetlands could be disastrous.

Finally, it should be noted that the British forces were in complete disarray, some uselessly throwing away their weapons, and a large number were undisciplined and drunk.

This report was created on 28th June 1940.

General Sir Harold E. Franklyn C.B.

Divisional Commander, Dunkirk.

12th July 1940

Second report dated 25th November 1940.

Marked SECRET

Once again, a report has surfaced that is very far from the truth. It concerns the BATTLE OF BRITAIN from 8th August 1940 to 31st October 1940.

The newspaper reports put out by our propaganda services suggest that the Spitfire piloted with young British pilots reported as "the few" from upper-crust homes were responsible for winning the Battle of Britain. The facts are very different. Only 180 pilots were educated privately, the overwhelming majority were "blue collar". Furthermore, over 20% were from other nationalities – Canadian, Czech, French, North African, Dutch, American, and most significantly Polish.

The Germans reported that during the invasion of Poland, all enemy aircraft had been destroyed on the ground, but enough took off to cost the Luftwaffe nearly 200 aircraft before the surrender. The Polish pilots arrived in Britain battle-hardened, as borne out by the fact that the Polish 303 Squadron took down more enemy planes than any other squadron during the battle. They were also too savvy to allow their planes to be armed according to RAF conventions, which 'seeded' the last 25 rounds to tip off the pilot that he was running out of ammunition. This of course gave the enemy the same message. Once they had run out of ammunition, they attempted to ram the German planes from the rear, in the safe knowledge that if they had to bail out, they could do so within the boundaries of the United Kingdom.

Most reports indicate that the Spitfire was the leading airplane, but it was, in fact, the Hurricane that did the most damage to the Luftwaffe, even though, 41% of Hurricanes were produced against 59% of Spitfires. The Hurricane was easier to patch up, after battle, as it was constructed of frame and fabric whereas the Spitfire was all metal. More importantly, it took 26 minutes to re-arm a Spitfire and only 9 minutes for a Hurricane. Although the Spitfire was faster, more manoeuvrable, and had a higher ceiling, it had a disadvantage against the Messerschmitt b109, the latter having fuel injection which prevented it from losing power when climbing. The Hurricane accounted for 1,593 enemy planes during the Battle of Britain, out of 2,739 German planes, almost two-thirds of the total.

The British public was led to believe that the 'few' were vastly outnumbered by around 3 to 1. This is not true, the British grossly overestimated the size of the Luftwaffe, and the latter suffered from the opposite illusion. At Dunkirk, Britain lost 300 fighters, leaving 700 to face the oncoming onslaught. By 9th August 1940, Britain had 1.456 fighters to the Luftwaffe, 1,011. By the end of the Battle of Britain, the RAF production far exceeded their losses, which the Germans were incapable of maintaining. Both sides reported huge losses for the other side, but actual figures for the RAF during the Battle were 1,535 and the Luftwaffe 2,662. Between August and September 1940 alone, the British lost 201 pilots and 493 planes to the Luftwaffe 1,132 aircrew and 862 planes.

The implication given to the British public was that if we lost the air war, Hitler could easily invade. This was complete nonsense, and Hitler knew it from the start and was never serious about an invasion. Air supremacy was desirable for many reasons, but the Germans knew that command of the skies would not seriously impede the ability of the Royal Navy to scupper any invasion force. As was proved later in the Battle of Crete, where over six thousand German Mountain Troops sailing in barges from the South of Greece, were sent to the bottom of the Mediterranean: only 600 reached Crete by sea. A destroyer could overturn an invasion barge by the wash it created.

Britain had 40 destroyers in the channel area to 2 German destroyers. Apart from radar, which the Germans initially underestimated, we had also cracked enemy codes (Ultra) which gave us all troop and ship movements in the channel area.

Note: It has been ordered by the Prime Minister, Winston Churchill, that all copies of these reports should be 'buried'.

I have literally followed the Prime Minister's instructions with both reports.

Signed,

Major-**General** Sir Edward Louis **Spears**, 1st Baronet, Bt, KBE, CB, MC.

1st December 1940

Note: It may be that someone may find this report and that the truth will eventually be told.

Note: What does the above tell you?

What is written in newspapers, on the web, or in bulletins given out by governments is not necessarily true, indeed, one wonders if any are.

Most of my books are written on such reported stories, which are often obtuse or incomplete. Using my lifetime experience, I look behind the news to try and assess what really happened. The Crowley Affair, although set mainly during five years after 1910, indicates two events in history that have never been divulged. The Shanghai Incident suggests why MH 370 and MH 17 were brought down and why they were connected. The Gorazde Incident indicates why the war came to a sudden end. The Moscow Assassin starts with the ex-Russian Minister, Boris Nemtsov, who was murdered by the Russian state. He was Jewish and that led to a complex retaliation, causing Putin extreme embarrassment. The Castrators offer a method of dealing with Boko Haram, the kidnappers of 300 schoolgirls. The current book, The Scottish Prerogative is a future indication of Russia financing Scotland to break away from the Union, this to happen under a socialist government.

IS YOUR MONEY SAFE?

"Beware the investment sirens, gold is the only safe policy
providing you can a. Keep it safe, and b. Carry it"

CHAPTER
26

---

*This story suggests you save your assets in your
own vault.*

Debt is the scourge of the modern currency system as
it is no longer pegged to the value of a commodity, such as
gold. The United States is the highest debtor in the G20 at
104% of GDP and the not far behind the UK at 87%. The
government debt equals £28,387 per person. In addition,
personal unsecured debt (minus mortgages) is running at
£15,983. All the figures mentioned are 2017 figures and have
continued to rise and are still rising.

How does this affect you? Debt is expensive, and due
to our monetary system, which is based on printing money,
more and more people are being led into ever-increasing
financial problems. Politically, this is a bomb ready to blow,
and worryingly there are similarities to the 1930's. The rise
of populist governments, the dissatisfaction with the gap

between the rich and the poor, the dissociation and dissatisfaction with politics. The unfair distribution of wealth.

Is your money safe on the property? Are your investments safe? Will you have enough money to live on, if the benefit system breaks down, as it already has for thousands of British families, now experiencing more and more moving into poverty?

The last crash was due to unsafe property loans fuelled by too many houses being built on spec, which were parcelled together and sold as investments they were called CDW's (Credit Default Swaps). This allowed people to take on debt that they could not afford and when the bubble burst, the owners of the equity threw people out of their homes, instead of coming to an arrangement to reduce the repayments, thus accelerating the problem, as empty houses soon deteriorate.

Now we are looking at a similar problem, but this time it is the financing of motor vehicles. The motor

industry is suffering, having tooled up for the building of diesel motor cars, as encouraged by the government, they now find that the vehicles they are producing are unpopular and the indication is that they will lose value at a much higher rate.

To overcome this problem, motor vehicles are being financed in a similar way to property in the USA in 2008. The loans are cheap, the discounts are large, and the amount offered for your old car is greater than normal. Sounds a good deal. Well, consider this, the loans are being parcelled up in the same way that houses were, except they are now termed ABS (Automobile Batch Subprime) instead of CDW.

These subprime loans move the risk from the Auto companies and finance corporations in the same way as happened with property in 2008. These consolidated loans are being snapped up by banks, corporations, insurance companies, pension funds, and the like. The security is nebulous, to say the least. There are no official figures for the UK, but in the USA, Americans owe over 1 trillion in auto loans. 40% of the population have auto loans, unbelievably 37% is already in subprime loans.

When there is a crash, the rich have an economic problem, but when it hits the poor, it becomes a political problem. This time it will be the weakest number in our society that will be hit, and the fallout will be substantially worse than 2008.

So, what should you do to protect your financial health? At the very least, review your investments and think about what could be adversely affected by a major crash equal to or worse than the 1930's. If in doubt move your wealth into cash, but not more than £100,000 in any one bank. Banks, even if they go bust, are protected. Subtly stock up in your freezer and tinned goods. Watch your daily news and buy the Financial Times regularly, watch out for signs of financial problems. **They are coming, you have been warned.** For those of you with financial advisors, be aware that these people, however honest and upstanding they may be, get paid for their advice and often receive commissions from the investment companies they deal with. Thus, their advice may not be entirely in your interest.

SPANISH TREASURE

"Keep digging".

CHAPTER
27

> *This story is fiction, except that I really do have the Spanish coins, and they were dug up in a garden in Kinsale.*

Enzo Gonzales was the Captain of the good ship Maria Esantes sailing out of Cartegena in Spain. He was on his way home from stealing a large amount of treasure from Caracas in South America, when he noticed a British Frigate on his tail. The British ship was south of him to windward, and so he decided to head north to the Irish Sea. Unfortunately for him, a storm was brewing, and his ship was swept onto the rocks just outside the Head of Kinsale in Southern Island. Enzo was a survivor, but he only managed to get ashore with a bag filled with silver loot, all his crew and the rest of the treasure were lost.

Making his way to the town of Kinsale, and speaking broken English, he managed to get to a hostelry managed by the catholic nuns. Being a staunch Catholic himself, he elicited their help, and managed to purchase a small property, which he turned into an Inn, subsequently called the Spanish Inn just across the water from Saint James Fort, one of the British forts guarding the entrance to Kinsale town. The other Bastian was Charles Fort on the same side of the water as the Inn. He planned to act as a spy for the

Spanish fleet which he knew had designs on landing on that part of Ireland, as the Spaniards were still smarting from being beaten at the Battle of Kinsale some years previously.

Although Enzo had a wife and children in Cartegena, he decided to find a wife in Ireland, and by paying a small sum to the nuns, he bought an attractive wench who was in service to the local nunnery, they were glad to see the back of her as proved difficult to control. Enzo soon found that the Irish woman was not the compliant girl he had married back in Spain, and he became more and more frustrated with her attitude and frequent bouts of bad temper, which he duly beat her for. His treasure was kept in a secret place, but on finding his new wife had found it and pilfered some of the cash, he gave the girl a good beating and decided to bury it in his garden. Getting a spade, he dug a large hole and as he was putting the treasure in, which was now contained in a tin. His wife crept up behind him and hit him hard on the back of the head with a hurling stick, knocking him unconscious. Unfortunately for her, the tin was already in the hole, and he fell on top of it. He was far too heavy for her to pull him out, so she simply shovelled the earth back on top of the still unconscious body. Afterwards, she took control of the Inn and did very well due to a catastrophic fire at the nunnery where she once worked. She immediately offered rooms to the nuns, rooms, which were reputed to be the most expensive in the whole of Ireland. On his deathbed, the man who started the fire, told the priest giving his last rites, that he had been paid by the female innkeeper to destroy the nunnery in revenge for the treatment she suffered while working there.

In 1995, my next-door neighbour was digging in his garden and found a skeleton. When it was removed, he found the casket of coins. He knew that I had travelled widely, so he gave some to me and asked if I could value them, but he died before I could do so – here they are...

WOMEN AT WAR

"Beware women scorned".

CHAPTER
28

This story is fiction.

Gabriel Steele was a prolific man, having sired 15 children with 4 wives and twice as many mistresses. At the age of 23, this had taken some doing. The problem was that he had no interest in supporting any of them and not a penny of his earnings went their way.

It was when the wives unexpectedly all met at a food bank one day, that was the beginning of his undoing. A plot was hatched, and Susie, Jenny, Anne, and Angela drew straws on who was going to carry out the final act. It was Jenny who drew the short straw. A 4-10 shotgun was brought from a farm, and later that week, the four found out that he was on holiday and would be at his home. They travelled to where he was living, and Jenny approached the door and rang the bell. There were many expletives inside the house, as he had been disturbed in his bed from his normal activity. He opened the door with just a T-shirt on, and everything else showing to the world. Jenny was just raising her gun and was about to squeeze the trigger, unaware that Gabriel's pet mongoose was in the garden. As everyone knows, Mongooses are killers of snakes, and unfortunately for Gabriel, his mongoose was getting on a bit and mistook the hanging appendage in front of him for a snake. It was not a pretty sight. Jenny realising that his prolific lifestyle was over, turned and quietly left without firing a shot.

The message in this story is that justice sometimes works in mysterious ways.

KITCHENER

"Beware the whom you hurt – revenge is sweet".

CHAPTER
29
True Story

After my return, I came to understand that the Axis powers lost despite their superior tactics, mainly because of technology, particularly the tank (thanks to the British navy under Churchill who took on the creation and testing of it) and the fact that Germany was not capable of surviving a war of attrition.

The Zimmerman Telegram, the secret diplomatic communication issued from the German Foreign Office in January 1917 proposing a military alliance, between Germany and Mexico almost certainly shortened the war, but it may not have had that effect it had, if Zimmerman had not admitted that he had sent it.

The British intelligence claimed that they had decoded it thus greatly enhancing their deductive powers. Of course, I knew the true story.

The revelation of the contents enraged Americans, especially after German Foreign Secretary Arthur Zimmerman publicly admitted on March 3 that the telegram was genuine, which helped generate support for the United States declaration of war on Germany in April. The decryption was described as the most significant intelligence triumph for Britain during World War I. One of the earliest occasions on which a piece of signal intelligence influenced world events.

Despite the overwhelming call for the Kaiser to be tried and hanged, George V kept his word, and the Kaiser was allowed to live in peace with his family in the Netherlands until the beginning of the Second World War. He died in 1940. His plan worked, thousands of lives on both sides were saved, and Germany was not occupied, which was his greatest fear but unfortunately, the French insisted on huge reparations which was to be the reason for the Second World War. Arguably it was the French that sowed the seeds possibly not realising the global monetary supply could not stand the financial drain. It was therefore France that were to suffer more than most in World War 2.

I was not to know it at the time, but Field Marshall Herbert Kitchener was killed shortly after I met him, in June 1915.

I referred to Kitchener as General when speaking to him, but he was a Field, Marshal. **Horatio Herbert Kitchener, 1st Earl Kitchener**, KG, KP, GCB, OM, GCSI, GCMG, GCIE, PC. Born on 24 June 1850 and was killed on 5 June 1916. He was a senior British Army officer and colonial administrator. He won notoriety for his Imperial campaigns, especially his scorched earth policy against the Boers and his establishment of concentration camps during the Second Boer War, and later played a central role in the early part of the First World War.

Kitchener was credited in 1898 to win the Battle of Omdurman and secure control of the Sudan for which he was made Baron Kitchener of Khartoum. As Chief of Staff (1900–1902) in the Second Boer War, he played a crucial role in Lord Roberts's conquest of the Boer Republics, and then succeeded Roberts as commander-in-chief. By that time, Boer forces had taken to guerrilla fighting, and British forces imprisoned Boer civilians in concentration camps. His term as Commander-in-Chief (1902–09) of the Army in India saw him quarrel with another eminent proconsul, the Viceroy Lord Curzon, who eventually resigned. Kitchener then returned to Egypt as a British Agent and Consul-General (*de facto* administrator).

In 1914, at the start of the First World War, Kitchener became Secretary of State for War, a cabinet minister. One of the few to foresee a long war, lasting for at least three years, and with the authority to act effectively on that perception, he organised the largest volunteer army that Britain had seen and oversaw a significant expansion of materiel production to fight on the Western Front. Despite having warned of the difficulty of provisioning for a long war. He was blamed for the shortage of shells in the spring of 1915. It was one of the events leading to the formation of a coalition government. And that stripped him of his control over munitions and strategy. Perhaps he was expecting a large shipment that was in the Lusitania when it sank?

On 5 June 1916, Kitchener was making his way to Russia on HMS *Hampshire* to attend negotiations with Tsar Nicholas II when the ship struck a German mine 1.5 miles (2.4 km) west of the Orkneys, Scotland, and sank. Kitchener was among 737 who died.

Deploying the BEF

At the War Council (5 August) Kitchener and Lieutenant-General Sir Douglas Haig argued that the BEF should be deployed at Amiens, where it could deliver a vigorous counter-attack once the German advance route was known. Kitchener argued that the deployment of the BEF in Belgium would result in having to retreat and abandon much of its supplies almost immediately. As the Belgian Army would be unable to hold its ground against the Germans;

Kitchener was proved right but given the belief in fortresses typical at the time, it is not surprising that the War Council disagreed with him.

Kitchener, believing Britain should husband her resources for a long war, decided at Cabinet (6 August) that the initial BEF would consist of only four infantry divisions (and one cavalry), not the 5 or 6 promised. His decision to hold back two of the six divisions of the BEF, was based on exaggerated concerns about the German invasion of Britain. He arguably saved the BEF from disaster as Sir John French (on the advice of Wilson who was much influenced by the French), might have been tempted to advance further into the teeth of the advancing German forces, had his force been more potent.

Kitchener's wish to concentrate further back at Amiens may also be influenced by a mostly accurate map of German dispositions published by Repington in *The Times* on the morning of 12 August. Kitchener had a three-hour meeting (12 August) with Sir John French, Murray, Wilson, and the French liaison officer Victor Huguet, before being overruled by the Prime Minister, who eventually agreed that the BEF should assemble at Maubeuge.

Sir John French's orders from Kitchener were to cooperate with the French but not take orders from them. Given that the tiny BEF (about 100,000 men, half of them serving regulars and half reservists) was Britain's only field army. Lord Kitchener also instructed French to avoid excessive losses and exposure to "forward movements where large numbers of French troops are not engaged" until Kitchener himself had had a chance to discuss the matter with the Cabinet.

Meeting with Sir John French
The BEF commander, Sir John French, concerned at heavy British losses at the Battle of Le

Cateau, was considering withdrawing his forces from the Allied line. By 31 August French Commander-in-chief Joffre, President Poincaré (relayed via Bertie, the British Ambassador), and Kitchener sent him messages urging him not to do so. Kitchener, authorised by a midnight meeting of whichever Cabinet Ministers could be found, left for France for a meeting with Sir John on 1 September.

Together with Viviani (French Prime Minister) and Millerand (now French War Minister), they met. Huguet recorded that Kitchener was "calm, balanced, reflective" whilst Sir John was "sour, impetuous, with congested face, sullen and ill-tempered". On Bertie's advice, Kitchener dropped his intention of inspecting the BEF. French and Kitchener moved to a separate room, and no independent account of the meeting exists. After the meeting, Kitchener telegraphed the Cabinet that the BEF would remain in the line, although taking care not to be outflanked, and told French to consider this "an instruction". French had a friendly exchange of letters with Joffre.

French had been furious that Kitchener had arrived wearing his field marshal's uniform. This was how Kitchener usually dressed at the time (Hankey thought Kitchener's uniform disrespectful, but it had probably not occurred to him to change). Still, French felt that Kitchener implied that he was his military superior and not merely a cabinet member. By the end of the year, French thought that Kitchener had "gone mad" and his hostility had become common knowledge at GHQ and GQG.

1915

In January 1915, Field Marshal Sir John French, the British Expeditionary Force commander, with the concurrence of other senior commanders (e.g., General Sir Douglas Haig), wanted the New Armies incorporated into existing divisions as battalions rather than sent out as entire divisions. French felt (wrongly) that the war would be over by the summer before the New Army divisions were deployed. As Germany had recently redeployed some divisions to the east and took the step of appealing to the Prime Minister, Asquith, over Kitchener's head, but Asquith refused to overrule Kitchener. This further damaged relations between French and Kitchener, who had travelled to France in September 1914 during the First Battle of the Marne to order French to resume his place in the Allied line.

Kitchener warned the French in January 1915 that the Western Front was a siege line that could not be breached, in the context of Cabinet discussions about amphibious landings on the Baltic or North Sea Coast, or against Turkey. To find a way to relieve pressure on the Western Front, Lord Kitchener proposed an invasion of Alexandretta with the Australian and New Zealand Army Corps (ANZAC), New Army, and Indian troops. Alexandretta was an area with a large Christian population and was the strategic centre of the Ottoman Empire's railway network — its capture would have cut the empire in two. Yet he was instead eventually persuaded to support Winston Churchill's disastrous Gallipoli Campaign in 1915–1916. (Churchill's responsibility for this campaign failure is debated; for more information see David Fromkins's *A Peace to End All Peace*.) That failure combined with the Shell Crisis of 1915 – amidst press publicity engineered by Sir John French – dealt Kitchener's political reputation a heavy blow. Kitchener was popular with the public, so Asquith retained him in office in the new coalition government. Still, responsibility for munitions was moved to a new ministry headed by David Lloyd George. He was a skeptic about the tank, which is why it was developed under Churchill's Admiralty's auspices.

With the Russians being pushed back from

Poland, Kitchener thought the transfer of German troops west and Britain's possible invasion increasingly likely and told the War Council (14 May) that he was not willing to send the New Armies overseas. He wired French (16 May 1915) that he would send no more reinforcements to France until he was clear the German line could be broken but sent two divisions at the end of May to please Joffre, not because he thought a breakthrough possible. He had wanted to conserve his New Armies to strike a knock-out blow in 1916–17, but by the summer of 1915 realised that high casualties and a major commitment to France were inescapable. "Unfortunately, we have to make war as we must, and not as we should like" he told the Dardanelles Committee on 20 August 1915.

At an Anglo-French conference at Calais (6 July) Joffre and Kitchener, who were opposed to "too vigorous" offensives, reached a compromise on "local offensives on a vigorous scale", and Kitchener agreed to deploy New Army divisions to France. An inter-Allied conference at Chantilly (7 July, including Russian, Belgian, Serb, and Italian delegates) agreed on coordinated offensives. however, Kitchener now came to support the upcoming Loos Offensive. He travelled to France for talks with Joffre and Millerand (16 August). The French leaders believed Russia might sue for peace (Warsaw had fallen on 4 August). Kitchener (19 August) ordered the Loos Offensive to proceed, despite the attack being on the ground not favoured by the French or Haig (then commanding First Army). The Official History later admitted that Kitchener hoped to be appointed Supreme Allied Commander. Liddell Hart speculated that this was why he allowed himself to be persuaded by Joffre. New Army divisions first saw action at Loos in September 1915.

REDUCTION IN POWERS

Kitchener continued to lose favour with politicians and professional soldiers. He found it "repugnant and unnatural to have to discuss military secrets with a large number of gentlemen with whom he was but barely acquainted". Esher complained that he would either lapse into "obstinacy and silence" or else mull aloud over various difficulties. Milner told Gwynne (18 August 1915) that he thought Kitchener, was a "slippery fish". By autumn 1915, with Asquith's Coalition close to breaking up over conscription, he was blamed for his opposition to that measure. (Which would eventually be introduced for single men in January 1916). And for the excessive influence that civilians like Churchill and Haldane had come to exert over strategy, allowing *ad hoc* campaigns to develop in Sinai, Mesopotamia, and Salonika. Generals such as Sir William Robertson were critical of Kitchener's failure to ask the General Staff. (Whose chief James Wolfe-Murray was intimidated by Kitchener) to study the feasibility of any of these campaigns.

Kitchener advised the Dardanelles Committee (21 October) that Baghdad be seized for the sake of prestige and then abandoned as logistically untenable. His advice was no longer accepted without question, but the British forces were eventually besieged and captured at Kut.

Archibald Murray (Chief of the Imperial General Staff) later recorded that Kitchener was "quite unfit for the position of secretary of state" and "impossible", claiming that he never assembled the Army Council as a body, but instead gave them orders separately, and was usually exhausted by Friday. Kitchener was also keen to break up Territorial units whenever possible whilst ensuring that "No "K" Division left the country incomplete". Murray wrote that "He seldom told the absolute the truth and the whole truth" and claimed that it was not until he left on a tour of inspection of Gallipoli and the Near East that Murray was able to inform the Cabinet that volunteering had fallen far below the level needed to maintain a BEF of 70 divisions, requiring the introduction of conscription. The Cabinet insisted on proper General Staff papers being presented in Kitchener's absence.

Asquith, who told Robertson that Kitchener was "an impossible colleague" and "his veracity left much to be desired", hoped that he could be persuaded to remain in the region as Commander-in-Chief and acted in charge of the War Office, but Kitchener took his seals of office with him so he could not be sacked in his absence. Douglas Haig – at that time involved in intrigues to have Robertson appointed Chief of the Imperial General Staff – recommended that Kitchener be appointed Viceroy of India ("where trouble was brewing") but not to the Middle East, where his strong personality would have led to that sideshow receiving too much attention and resources. Kitchener visited Rome and Athens, but Murray warned that he would likely demand the diversion of British troops to fight the Turks in the Sinai.

Kitchener and Asquith agreed that Robertson should become CIGS, but Robertson refused to do this if Kitchener "continued to be his own CIGS", although given Kitchener's great prestige he did not want him to resign; he wanted the Secretary of State to be side-lined to an advisory role like the Prussian War Minister. Asquith asked them to negotiate an agreement, which they did over the exchange of several draft documents at the Hotel de Crillon in Paris. Kitchener agreed that Robertson alone should present strategic advice to the Cabinet, with Kitchener responsible for recruiting and supplying the Army, although he refused to agree that military orders should go out over Robertson's signature alone – it was agreed that the Secretary of State should continue to sign orders jointly with the CIGS. The agreement was formalised in a Royal Order in Council in January 1916. Robertson was suspicious of efforts in the Balkans and Near East and was instead committed to major British offensives against Germany on the Western Front — the first of these was to be the Somme in 1916.

1916

Early in 1916, Kitchener visited Douglas Haig, newly appointed Commander-in-Chief of the BEF in France. Kitchener had been a key figure in the removal of Haig's predecessor Sir John French, with whom he had a poor relationship. Haig differed with Kitchener over the importance of Mediterranean efforts and wanted to see a strong General Staff in London, but nonetheless valued Kitchener as a military voice against civilians' folly such as Churchill. however, he thought Kitchener "pinched, tired, and much aged", and thought it sad that his mind was "losing its comprehension" as the time for a decisive victory on the Western Front (as Haig and Robertson saw it) approached. Kitchener was doubtful of Haig's plan to win a decisive victory in 1916 and would have preferred smaller and purely attrition attacks, but sided with Robertson in telling the Cabinet that the planned Anglo-French Offensive on the Somme should go ahead.

Kitchener was under pressure from French Prime Minister Aristide Briand (29 March 1916) for the British to attack the Western Front to help relieve the stress of the German attack at Verdun. The French refused to bring troops home from Salonika, which Kitchener thought was a play for the increase of French power in the Mediterranean.

On 2 June 1916, Lord Kitchener personally answered questions asked by politicians about his running of the war effort; at the start of hostilities, Kitchener had ordered two million rifles from various US arms manufacturers. Only 480 of these rifles had arrived in the UK by 4 June 1916. The number of shells supplied was no less paltry. Kitchener explained the efforts he had made to secure alternative supplies. He received a resounding vote of thanks from the 200 Members of Parliament who had arrived to question him, both for his candour and for his efforts to keep the troops armed; Sir Ivor Herbert, who, a week before, had introduced the failed vote of censure in the House of Commons against Kitchener's running of the War Department, personally seconded the motion.

In addition to his military work, Lord Kitchener contributed to efforts on the home front. The knitted sock patterns of the day used a seam up the toe that could rub uncomfortably against the toes. Kitchener encouraged British and American women to knit for the war effort and contributed a sock pattern featuring a new technique for a seamless join of the toe, still known as the Kitchener stitch.

RUSSIAN MISSION
During his other political and military concerns, Kitchener devoted personal attention to the Eastern Front's deteriorating situation. This included the provision of extensive stocks of war materiel for the Russian armies, which had been under increasing pressure since mid-1915 In May 1916 the Chancellor of the Exchequer Reginald Mckenna suggested that Kitchener head a special and confidential mission to Russia to discuss munition shortages, military strategy and financial difficulties with the Imperial Russian Government and the *Stavka* (military high command),

which was now under the personal command of Tsar Nicholas II. Both Kitchener and the Russians were in favour of face-to-face talks and a formal invitation from the Tsar was received on 14 May. Kitchener with a party of officials, military aides, and personal servants left London by train for Scotland on the evening of 4 June.

Death

Lord Kitchener sailed from Scrabster to Scapa Flow on 5 June 1916 aboard HMS *Oak* before transferring to the armoured cruiser HMS *Hampshire* for his diplomatic mission to Russia. At the last minute, Admiral Sir John Jellicoe changed the *Hampshire's* route based on a misreading of the weather forecast and ignoring (or not being aware of) recent German intelligence and sightings of U-boat activity in the vicinity of the amended route. Shortly before 19:30 hours the same day, steaming for the Russian port of Arkhangelsk during a Force 9 gale, *Hampshire* struck a mine laid by the newly launched German U-boat *U-75* (commanded by Curt Beitzen) and sank west of the Orkney Islands. Recent research has set the death toll of those aboard *Hampshire* at 737. Only twelve survived. Amongst the dead were all ten members of his entourage. Kitchener was seen standing on the quarterdeck during the approximately twenty minutes that it took the ship to sink. His body was never recovered.

The news of Kitchener's death was received with shock all over the British Empire. A man in Yorkshire committed suicide at the word; a sergeant on the Western Front was heard to exclaim "Now we've lost the war. Now we've lost the war"; and a nurse wrote home to her family that she knew Britain would win as long as Kitchener lived, and now that he was gone: "How awful it is – a far worse blow than many German victories. So long as he was with us, we knew even if things were gloomy that his guiding hand was at the helm."

General Douglas Haig commanding the British Armies on the Western Front remarked on first receiving the news of Kitchener's death via a German radio signal intercepted by the British Army, "How shall we get on without him." King George V wrote in his diary: It is indeed a heavy blow to me and a great loss to the nation and the allies. He ordered army officers to wear black armbands for a week.

C. P. Scott, the editor of *The Manchester Guardian*, is said to have remarked that "as for the old man, he could not have done better than to have gone down, as he was a great impediment lately."

Conspiracy theories

Kitchener's great fame, the suddenness of his death, and its apparently convenient timing for several parties gave almost immediate rise to a few conspiracy theories about his death. One was posited by Lord Alfred Douglas (of Oscar Wilde fame), positing a connection between Kitchener's death, the recent naval Battle of Jutland, Winston Churchill, and a Jewish conspiracy. Churchill successfully sued Douglas in what proved to be the last successful case of criminal libel in British legal history, and the latter spent six months in prison. Another claimed that the *Hampshire* did not strike a mine at all but was sunk by explosives secreted in the vessel by Irish Republicans.

In 1926, a hoaxer named Frank Power claimed in the *Sunday Referee* newspaper that a Norwegian fisherman had found Kitchener's body. Power brought a coffin back from Norway and prepared it for burial in St Pauls Cathedral. At this point, however, the authorities intervened, and the coffin was opened in the presence of police and a distinguished pathologist. The box was found to contain only tar for weight. There was widespread public outrage at Power, but he was never prosecuted.

FBI file photo of Duquesne

General Erich Ludendorff, General quartier Meister, and joint head (with von Hindenburg) of the Germanys war effort stated in the 1920s that Russian communists working against the Tsar had betrayed the plan to visit the Russians to the German command. His account was that Kitchener was "killed because of his ability" as he feared he would help the tsarist Russian Army recover.

Frederick Joubert Duquesne, a Boer soldier and spy, claimed that he had assassinated Kitchener after an earlier attempt to kill him in Cape Town failed. He was arrested and court-martialed in Cape Town and sent to the penal colony of Bermuda, but managed to escape to the U.S. MI5 confirmed that Duquesne was "a German intelligence officer ... involved in a series of acts of sabotage against British shipping in South American waters during the First World war"; he was wanted for: "murder on the high seas, the sinking and burning of British ships, the burning of military stores, warehouses, coaling stations, conspiracy, and the falsification of Admiralty documents."

Duquesne's story was that he returned to Europe, posed as the Russian Duke Boris Zakrevsky in 1916, and joined Kitchener in Scotland. While on board HMS *Hampshire* with Kitchener, Duquesne signalled a German submarine that then sank the cruiser, and was rescued by the submarine, later being awarded the Iron

Cross for his efforts. Duquesne was later apprehended and tried by the authorities in the U.S. for insurance fraud but managed to escape again.

In the Second World War, he ran a German spy ring in the United States until the FBI caught him in what became the biggest round-up of spies in U.S. history: the *Duquesne Spy Ring*. Coincidentally, Kitchener's brother was to die in office in Bermuda in 1912, and his nephew, Major H.H.

Hap Kitchener, who had married a Bermudian, purchased (with a legacy left to him by his uncle) Hinson's Island, part of former Prisoner of War camp from which Duquesne had escaped, after the First World War as the location of his home and business.

Nothing I read later, changed my opinion of Kitchener, a soldier who lived and fought the old way but was incapable of assessing and using new technology. His biggest problem being the difficulty in dealing with his political masters. It should be a lesson for us.

There is a sequel to the above story in that the family of Duquesne was taken to one of the British Concentration camps in South Africa, where they died of disease and starvation. The soldier who created the camps was Kitchener. It is not impossible that Dusquesne planned his revenge which was consummated in the North Sea with the death of the man responsible thus killing two birds with one stone.

CHAPTER
30

The winner collects the spoils.
True Story
When the Armistice was signed on 11 November 1918, conditions of the agreement demanded the entire German U-boat fleet be surrendered and confiscated immediately.

However, the Allies had not yet decided what to do with the surface ships of the German High Seas Fleet.

It was decided that they should be interned in Allied or neutral ports until their fate could be agreed upon during peace negotiations.

British Admiral Sir David Beatty presented the terms of the surrender to German Rear Admiral Hugo Meurer and other officers aboard his flagship, the battleship HMS Queen Elizabeth on the night of 15 - 16 November 1918.

As Commander-in-Chief of the Royal Navy's Grand Fleet, Beatty oversaw ensuring the surrender of 74 German ships for internment, checking they had been disarmed, and escorting them to be laid up.

This mission was codenamed Operation ZZ.

Admiral Franz Ritter von Hipper, commander of the German fleet, refused to hand his ships over to Beatty, and delegated this task to Rear Admiral Ludwig von Reuter.

On 19 November, the fleet of German warships led by von Reuter in his flagship, the battleship Friedrich der Grösse, left Germany to rendezvous with Beatty's ships in the North Sea.

At the rendezvous, the ships formed up as required and the joint convoy of 191 Allied and 70 German vessels that sailed into the Firth of Forth, Scotland, on 21 November 1918 was the largest fleet of warships ever assembled.

Once all the German ships had dropped anchor, Beatty gave the signal that the German flag was to be hauled down at sunset and not to be raised again without permission - a controversial move given the ships remained the property of Germany during internment.

Once checks that disarmament had been carried out had been completed, the German ships sailed under heavy Allied escort between 25 – 27 November for internment at the massive natural harbour at Scapa Flow in the Orkney Islands.

Three more ships would join them a short time after, and the 74th and final ship to arrive was the flagship of the High Seas Fleet, the dreadnought battleship Baden in January 1919, fulfilling the 74 ships required according to the terms of the internment.

For Rear Admiral von Reuter, command of his fleet was a difficult task from the outset.

Many among his crews had experienced long periods of inactivity since the Battle of Jutland in 1916 and had been laid up in port on board the ships subsisting on limited rations caused by blockades.

With the end of the war in sight, in October 1918 Grand Admiral Reinhardt Scheer planned an unsanctioned operation to send his fleet to inflict as much damage to the Royal Navy as possible, arguing: 'There can be no future for a fleet fettered by a dishonourable peace.'

In other words, because Germany had not been defeated militarily, either on land or at sea, the navy should attempt a final attack to preserve its honour.

However, it was also hoped a successful mission may have changed the military position to prevent surrender entirely, or else ensure more favour for German sailors however, this was a suicide mission and one which would act only to extend the war, and they refused to follow orders to prepare for sea.

Protest and mutiny among sailors and industrial workers followed: a symptom of the broader problems the war and associated hardships had caused in Germany and elsewhere towards the end of the First World War.

This escalated into widespread revolt which resulted in the Socialists declaring Germany a republic on 9 November, followed by the exile and abdication of <u>Kaiser Wilhelm II</u>.

It comes as no surprise therefore, that von Reuter's already unenviable task of surrendering the fleet and commanding such despondent, unpredictable, and in some cases, revolutionary crews was made more difficult when his ships were sent to Scapa Flow for internment (a port which was not neutral as originally agreed, but also in a very remote location). Favourable Armistice terms.

Once at Scapa Flow most of von Reuter's 20,000 men were gradually sent back to Germany, leaving a small number aboard the ships as caretaker crews.

Those who remained now found themselves indeterminately stranded aboard their ships with a lack of supplies and no entertainment, which resulted in poor discipline and appalling living conditions.

A particularly troublesome group aboard von Reuter's flagship became so unmanageable that they caused him to seek permission from the British to make his flagship the cruiser Emden instead.

With no fresh meat supplies, and being forbidden to change ships or go ashore, the sailors sought their own recreation and food supplies.

Fishing was an ideal way to pass the time and supplement their diets, and on at least one German destroyer, the crew built a spring-loaded gun with which to kill seagulls to eat.

With the Paris Peace Conference discussions ongoing and the **Treaty of Versailles** delayed until the end of June 1919, the Allies remained divided over the fate of the ships.

Most wanted a share of their navies, but Britain wanted the ships to be scrapped to prevent other nations from gaining naval superiority.

By May the fate of the German fleet was still to be decided. However, the treaty did call for the surrender of the interned ships by 21 June.

On discovering this news, von Reuter planned to scuttle his fleet as he'd been ordered to in the event the ships were to be seized by the Allies.

Unknown to von Reuter, the deadline was subsequently extended to 23 June, and in anticipation of scuttling, Rear Admiral Sydney Fremantle, commander of the 1st Battle Squadron at Scapa Flow guarding the German ships, had planned to seize them on 23 June, However, on the morning of 21 June 1919, the British fleet left Scapa Flow for exercises, and von Reuter saw his chance.

He gave the order to scuttle, and his crews' opened seacocks, torpedo tubes, and portholes on the ships to flood them and once again hoisted their flags of the Imperial German Navy.

When the small British force left behind by Fremantle to guard the German ships realised what was happening, they informed the main fleet and attempted to save some of the ships.

However, only 22, including Emden, were successfully beached in shallow water.

Of the 74 German ships interned at Scapa Flow, 52 (or an equivalent of about 400,000 tons of material) were scuttled within five hours, representing the greatest loss of shipping in a single day in history.

This was also the day on which the final German casualties of the First World War were to be claimed, and although nobody drowned, nine sailors were shot and killed and sixteen were injured by the British during brawls when they refused to help save the ships.

Although von Reuter was accused of behaving without honour by a somewhat angry Fremantle before being taken prisoner along with almost 1,800 of his men, in Germany he was praised as the man who had preserved the honour of the High Seas Fleet.

He was released from imprisonment in Britain in 1920 and asked to resign as a naval officer a few months after his return to Germany due to the enforced reduction of the navy according to the Treaty of Versailles.

France and other Allied nations were furious at the scuttling because they wanted a share of the ships.

Britain joined in the condemnation. However, there were some, including Admiral Wemyss, the man who had suggested the internment in the first place, who considered it a relief, arguing:

'It disposes, once and for all, the thorny question of the redistribution of these ships.'

Salvage operations began in 1919 to remove the scuttled ships, which had prevented the use of piers and fishing stations and were a hazard to shipping.

In the years that followed, most of the ships were purchased from the Admiralty to be raised and scrapped by various private companies, the most prolific being Ernest Cox of Cox and Danks Ltd., who purchased 28 ships and a floating dock with which to raise them. This dock had been seized from Germany as part of reparations for the scuttling and enabled Cox to raise 26 destroyers and eventually, the battlecruiser Hindenburg in 1930.

Of the 52 ships scuttled in 1919, seven remain at the bottom of the sea today. They are registered under the Ancient Monuments and Archaeological Areas Act 1979 and provide some of the best shipwreck diving in Europe.

CHAPTER
31

An extraordinary man and a good friend
True Story

MY GOOD FRIEND JOHN GOLDS
FROM THE TIMES Tuesday 16th of June 2020 Obituaries

A colonial officer in Kenya who fought the Mau Mau, opened a cheese factory and was disappointed with the 'low' price on his head.

John Golds was furious. The price on his head was only £500 about £10,000 in today's money. '' I did think I was worth rather more than that,' ' he grumbled. Golds was the district commissioner in Wajir County, in northeast Kenya, in the months leading up to independence in 1963. '' I had to control an area the size of Great Britain with a staff of 200 regular police, 185 tribal police, and a camel corps of 35,' ' he recalled, adding that his beat included the 1,000-mile border with Somalia and Ethiopia, where there were frequent skirmishes. '' It was a real battle, and we were ambushed frequently.' '

On one rainy day, a border post was attacked, and Golds flew there in a single-engine aircraft to offer support. He was accompanied by six of his tribal police who had never flown before. '' As they landed, the plane turned upside down on the slick waterlogged strip,' ' he recalled. No had we extracted ourselves from the plane then we were attacked.' '

[Authors note: John told us when the plane landed upside down, he yelled to the police accompanying him not to unfasten their safety belts straight away as he was afraid some of them might end up with broken necks. When he extracted the men, he was told by the leading policeman that he enjoyed the flight but did not realise that the planes landed upside down. John then realised that they were not in a fit state to deal with the attackers and ran the 25 miles back to base. It was difficult for us to imagine the overweight he was when we knew he could run anywhere.]

It was not all firefighting. He legalised the use of the stimulant miraa. He established schooling for girls, many of whom were nomadic, and set up a maternity unit. Before long the mortality rate fell dramatically among mothers and their babies.

As the representative of the declining British Empire, he became something of a celebrity and was featured on CBS television and photographed by the American magazine under the headline '' A flag still flies in a setting sun.' ' He was a member of the Royal Wajir Yacht Club. a male-only ex-pat club where the dress code was a silly hat kikoy (sarong) worn with a tie. When John Profumo, the war minister, visited he was initiated into the club wearing his wife's hat. [Authors note: John Profumo did much more, he saw a calendar on the wall with scantily clothed girls and leafed through it, stopping at Christine Keeler and wrote across it '' This is mine' ' and put it back on the wall.

A month later the world press arrived for their annual inspection, although it was not so much an inspection but a slap-alcoholic up lunch. They flew off in the late afternoon and John sighed with relief.

They had been gone about 10 minutes when John's number 2 told John with some consternation that the girlie calendar had disappeared. They knew it was hung in the bar when the assembled press was having lunch so John radioed the pilot asking him if he would ask his co-pilot if he would retrieve it and bring it back on the next flight. Several minutes later the pilot radioed back and told John that all the passengers had denied taking it. John knew the future that such a document would cause if published, so he ordered the pilot to turn around and land Wajir. The pilot refused. '' In that case, as soon as you land at Nairobi airport, I will have you arrested, and as you are still in my flight plan area, your refusal to follow my instructions will forfeit your pilot᾽s licence. Needless to say, the pilot turned the aircraft around. They were greeted by 30 soldiers who quickly surrounded the plane and John went on board facing the now angry passengers. He shouted ‘’ I know the calendar was taken from the Wajir Yacht Club and if the person who took it won᾽t give it up, I will carry out a search with my assembled soldiers and they will find it. A passenger stood up and admitted that he had taken it as a joke. John thought it was taken by the Daily Mirror, but it was a journalist from the Times. It was retrieved and burnt outside the Yacht club. The plane, which contained the very unhappy journalist as his compatriots were very cross.]

Kenya gained independence in December 19630and Golds took a month᾽s leave, flying to Stockholm to indulge his love of opera. While for the curtain to rise at the Royal Swedish Opera he was summoned to take a call from Jomo Kenyatta, the new President of Kenya. ‘’ I was told my successor had been assassinated and my orders were to return to Kenya forthwith.’ ’ On his return, he learned of the price on his head. ‘’ Anyway, they had five goes at me,’ ’ he recalled. ‘’ And I am glad to say they missed.’ ’
John Malcolm Golds was born in South London in 1922, the only child of Sidney Golds and his wife, Gladys (nee Cruttenden). The family moved to Chipstead, Surrey, and he was educated at Whitgift School, Croydon, though they soon moved again. ‘’ Early [n the war my parents and I evacuated to Plymouth where a big naval base is located.’ ’ He told the author Cutting Loose: From Rat Race to Deam Lifestyles (1996). ‘’ We stayed there for a year until we were bombed out. Nothing had happened in London. We went back to London and then the massive bombings started. The rest of my early life was.
     spent in air shelters,’ ’

For his 18th birthday, he was given life membership of the East India Club St. James' s. He was offered a place at the // Scouts, the next dealt with health, the third on something entirely different. A huge range of subjects of subjects, neither of us knew anything about.' '

Having dealt with the aftermath of independence, Golds was invited in 1964 to join Sir Evelyn Baring, the former governor of Kenya, who had become chairman of the Development Commonwealth (CDC). ' ' Six weeks later I was in Guyana, South America,' ' He recalled. He spent three years managing Guyana Timbers before being promoted to comptroller for the Caribbean, covering 14 islands. ' ' I spent most of my time in a little plane flying all over the Caribbean and investing CDC monies to further economic development.' ' He said. One project he set in motion was the construction of a causeway linking Pigeon Island and Gros Islet in the North of Saint Lucia. By that time, he was engaged to Pamela Broadhead, an architect, but she was killed in an aircraft crash near Nairobi in 1969.

The following year he returned to Britain, where he acquired a flat overlooking the sea in Brighton and became the highest-paid office boy in London.

For his 18th birthday, he was given life membership of the East India Club in St James's. He was offered a place at the Royal (Dick) School of Veterinary Studies at Edinburgh University, but this was deferred for a couple of years to give priority to soldiers returning from the war. Instead, he joined Burroughs Welcome, the medical research company, as a lab assistant, but it didn't work out.

His father, who managed Shell's fleet of oil tankers from London, found him a crewing opportunity. Reaching Mombasa, Golds travelled upcountry to stay with a friend of his grandparents. He was hired as an assistant manager of a six-thousand-acre mixed farm, but when the manager left the 20-year-old Golds took over. With the farm remaining stubbornly unprofitable he borrowed £1,000, persuaded the farmer to invest a similar sum and together they started a factory producing cheese and canned milk. Doinyo Lessos Creameries in Eldoret, in the Rift Valley, continues to thrive. "My partner runs it," he said in the mid-nineties. "I go there twice a year to tell him how I think it should be done. But he does it his way and knows far better than I how to do it.

In 1952 the Mau Mau rebellion began against British rule. A state of emergency was declared, and a call was sent out for volunteers. Golds applied to be a district officer with the Kikuyu Guard, a government paramilitary force, and was based at Kiambu in the northern suburbs of Nairobi. On his first night, their station was attacked. In the dark, he was unable to find his rifle, which in any case he had orders not to use. Instead, he picked up a hammer to defend himself. The following months continued in a similar vein. "Ambushes were frequent," he recalled. "We were often shot at, I lost quite a few of my men, but survived myself without a scratch. But there were a lot of close calls."

Golds had been there for about six months when it became apparent that he was running the district while the British officer whose job it was spent much of his time socialising and was soon removed. Golds befriended members of the selection panel and was offered the post. He became involved in the country's programme of land consolidation, working out a system for consolidating small parcels of land, some of them only a few square feet, into practical-sized holdings. "I did this for two years and I measured up with my surveyors something like five million little pieces of land and converted them to about 200,000 title deeds," he recalled. In 1960he drove his brand-new

Ford Anglia to a cinema in Nairobi to watch Princess Margaret's wedding.

Golds also visited his factory, after stopping at The Stag's Head restaurant in Nakuru, northwest of Nairobi to have dinner "with a young aspiring politician." His friendship with Daniel Arap Moi (obituary February 5, 2020) who went on to be president from 1978 to 2002, was "not unhelpful in my life, "he said. For a short time, he was Moi's secretary, "I wrote speeches for him, sometimes three or four a day," Golds recalled. "One, say, was for the Boy Scouts, the next dealt with health, and the third on something entirely different. A huge range of subjects, which neither of us knew anything about."

Having dealt with the aftermath of independence, Golds was invited in 1964 to join Sir Evelyn Baring, the former governor of Kenya, who had become Chairman of the Commonwealth Development Corporation (CDC). "Six weeks later I was in Guyana, South America," he recalled. He spent three years managing Guyana Timbers before being promoted to comptroller for the Caribbean, covering 14 islands. "I spent most of my time in a little plane flying all over the Caribbean and investing CDC monies to further economic development," he said. One project he set in motion was the construction of a causeway linking Pidgeon Island and Gros Islet in the north of St Lucia.

By that time, he was engaged to Pamela Broadhead, an architect, but she was killed in an aircraft crash near Nairobi in 1969. The following year he returned to Britain, where he acquired a flat overlooking the sea in Brighton and "became the highest paid office boy in London", but within a few months had grown bored and took early retirement. His intention had been to return to the cheese factory in Kenya, but he was instead offered three positions in real estate back in the Caribbean, he accepted them all and appointed managers to run the day-to-day businesses. One was on Mustique, where he became friendly with Princess Margaret and many of the island's visiting celebrities. He ran his operations, which included the construction of retirement homes in the US, from an apartment at Rodney Bay, St Lucia, next to which was moored Lessos 111, his 46ft yacht.

Golds eventually retired to Kenya in 2007, settling at Bilgewater, the house set in ten acres of beachside bush on the coast of Watamy, north of Mombasa that he had bought in 1953. In pride of place was a plaque on the wall declaring his freedom of the City of London. Before long he had been drawn into reviving the moribund north coast branch of the Kenya Horticultural Society. His former life as a district commissioner caught up with him once in a taxi in Austin Texas. Realising that his driver was Somalian he inquired about the man's background and in his enthusiasm revealed his name and former position on the Kenya-Somalia border. The driver suddenly recognised him, hit the brakes, and reminded him that there was a price on his head, before adding "I suppose it's too late to cash it in now."

John Golds, MBE, a colonial officer, was born on September 6th, 1927. He died on June 12[th,] 2020, aged 92.

Printed in Great Britain
by Amazon

28279915R00136